W9-BMU-124

downpour

HE WILL COME TO US LIKE THE RAIN

downpour

JAMES MACDONALD

B&H
PUBLISHING GROUP
Nashville, Tennessee

ISBN: 978-0-8054-4199-4

Published by B & H Publishing Group
Nashville, Tennessee

Dewey Decimal Classification: 248.84
Subject Headings: SPIRITUAL GROWTH
                   CHRISTIAN LIFE

Unless otherwise indicated, the Bible quotations are from the Holy Bible, English Standard Version, copyright © 2001 by Crossway Bibles, a division of Good News Publishers. Other versions quoted are the Holman Christian Standard Bible (HCSB), copyright © 1999, 2000, 2002, 2003 by Holman Bible Publlishers, Nashville, Tennessee; the New American Standard Bible (NASB), copyright © 1960, 1962, 1963, 1968, 1971, 1972, 1973, 1975, 1977, 1995 by the Lockman Foundation; the New King James Version (NKJV), copyright © 1982 by Thomas Nelson, Inc.; and the New International Version (NIV), copyright © 1973, 1978, 1984 by International Bible Society.

08 09 10 11 12   15 14 13 12 11 10 9 8 7

To the followers of Jesus known as
Harvest Bible Chapel
for your resolute determination
to have more of God in your life
and your unflinching readiness
to follow the biblical path to personal revival.

By God's grace we have many amazing years ahead
under the clouds of mercy.

Contents

Before You Begin

Warning: This introduction is longer than ones you'll find in most books, but please do not proceed without reading it. I believe that life is too short to waste time reading or writing books that only entertain. This is a book to change your life. If that is to happen, you have to fully understand and commit to the journey that we are beginning together. Set aside at least an hour to read this introduction, and if you fully engage . . . the sky is the limit. If you do not . . . well, put it on the shelf with the rest of the books you had high hopes for.

What Kind of Book Is This?

What is your favorite kind of road map? Now there's a question I bet you've never considered. Do you like the big fold-out kind that gives you the lay of the land? Do you prefer the books filled with little maps of every place imaginable? Are you fond of maps that make travel enjoyable by adding cartoons and captions about fun places to investigate? What's your favorite kind of map?

Maybe you're thinking, *Hey James, I like the kind of map that helps me find my way. I don't need a map to be my friend or give me warm fuzzies. I just want a map that is clear, so I can get where I am going without getting lost.* Good! I totally agree.

In view of this, then, tell me: What's your favorite kind of recipe? Since I'm not much of a cook, I'm unsure how you are going to answer that question. Do you like books filled with pictures that show the meal you're making at every step in the process?

> You are headed toward an encounter with God that will flood your soul with joy in a way that eclipses anything you might have previously called satisfaction.

Do you like recipes that go into great detail about every ingredient, telling you where to find them in their purest form and how to store them? Maybe you like a book where each individual recipe tells the history of the person who created the recipe, how it's cooked around the world, and a scratch and sniff in the back so you know what aroma will fill your kitchen. Again, if you're tracking with me you're getting a bit weary. You may be thinking, *What's wrong with this guy? I like recipes that teach how to make the meal in the fewest words possible, one picture maximum. I don't want to invest the next year learning about a single meal. I want a recipe that gets me successfully from kitchen to dining room in the fewest steps and the shortest time possible.*

Is that what you think? If you do, you may feel how I often do when I read a book. Why can't books be like maps and recipes? As in, this is the goal and this is how to get there.

What if there *was* a book like that?

What if there was a book that didn't try to entertain you with funny stories and a picture on every page?

What if there was a book about a subject so critical and a need so urgent that it cut past the endless allegory and sincere attempts at keeping your attention?

What if there was a book that laid out the critical information with the simplicity of a map and the clarity of a recipe card?

What if there was a book so concerned about your life in this moment that it made no attempt to make you feel good, but rather reached out like a lifeguard in an emergency and freed you from what your soul has been wallowing in for so long?

Solomon probably said with a sigh, **Of making many books there is no end** (Ecclesiastes 12:12). In the United States alone, there are thousands of book companies publishing more than one and one-half million titles each year. We need another book like we need a hole in the head. What we're dying for is a clear, simple recipe—a road map back to God. So let's cut the *blah, blah, blah* and get at it. Are you with me?

You are headed toward an encounter with God that will flood your soul with joy in a way that eclipses anything you might have previously called satisfaction. You might be thinking, *This sounds pretty amazing, James. Does this really happen to people?* Yes, it really does. That's why we'll interrupt our discussion in each chapter with little commercials called "Pictures of Personal Revival" about real people in history and the Bible who experienced a downpour of personal revival. It happened to them—and it can happen to you.

Don't Waste Your Time—Find Out If This Book Is for You!

In a lawn chair at the front of our church's main entrance is a guy who's been sitting there for months. He started coming every morning this summer. He sat there while the autumn leaves blew around him, and I saw him there again this morning as the snow swirled, covering his feet. Across his chest he wears a big sign that reads OBSERVER. And that's all he does. He sits there—observing.

He's not some wacko; he's actually doing a legitimate job. We're building a new worship center. As countless trucks come and go each week through that main entrance, delivering steel and other building supplies, he sits and watches. This "observer" monitors construction traffic to ensure that non union trucks don't pass his entrance. At least that's what he's supposed to do. In reality, he sleeps or reads or stares into space. Somewhere along the line he moved from function to form. Now he's like an unplugged toaster that looks the part but is more window dressing than union security.

> *If you wake up one morning and find yourself in a desert, then you must trace your steps back to where you up and wandered away. You've got to return to the Lord.*

As you might guess, this "observer" has been the source of many puzzled looks and the brunt of some jokes among our church staff. Someone propped a stuffed scarecrow in the "observer's" place on Halloween. Nobody noticed the difference until midafternoon. We've had a lot of fun with it.

But I'll tell you what's not funny—when that "form without function" mentality moves from the street to the worship center. This is a book for people who have become spiritual *observers*. If you are unhappy with your current state of spiritual hunger; if you feel like your love for God has grown cold—then hard—to God's people and God's Word; if God has moved from the passion of your life to the back burner; if instead of straining for more of God—to put Him first and receive His best—you find yourself unexplainably holding back; and if you feel any of these things in increasing measure, this is definitely the book for you. This is a book about personal revival.

What Do We Mean by Revival?

The Bible teaches clearly and repeatedly that God wants to *revive* our relationship with Him. Revival is *renewed interest after a period of indifference or decline.* He wants to wake us up, to refresh our faith—to fire us up again.

If you feel like your faith is a bit off course, you must know that the first wrong turn in our lives is always a move *away* from God. If you wake up one morning and find yourself in a desert, then you must trace your steps back to where you up and wandered away. You've got to return to the Lord. This kind of pain that won't go away is rooted in a failure of faith, and all pleasure flows from unplugging the fountain of joy that is found only in God.

What Revival Isn't

Sadly, when you say the word *revival* today, people think of all the circus chicanery and religious nonsense that accompanies flesh-induced spiritual fervor. For that reason I must spend a moment explaining what I *don't* mean by revival.

Revival is *not* long lines of anxious sinners waiting for a turn at the microphone to reveal their most secret sinful something. That's not revival.

Revival is *not* emotional extravagance where people are caught up in the moment and fall down, act bizarrely, unbiblically, and out of control. That's not revival.

The Bible does not invite us to seek a revival, ask God for a revival, or pray that revival will come. In fact, the Bible does not even use the specific word *revival,* though it frequently talks about people being revived. Throughout history there have been some downpours of God's blessing that people called "revival," but we don't have control over moves of God that affect entire cities or regions. What we can affect is the experience of "being revived" personally.

Don't Get the Cart before the Horse

Don't attempt to be revived if you have never been *vived* in the first place. Can you tell a story like this?

> There was a time in my life when I was going the wrong way, and the Lord reached out and brought me to the cross. By faith I experienced the forgiveness of sin that Jesus died and rose again to provide. At that time my eyes were opened, my heart was gripped, my life was captured by the grace of God; and I have never been the same since.

That is the story of every person who has been *vived*, or given life in Christ. Second Corinthians 5:17 says that if any of us is in **Christ, he is a new creation; the old has gone, the new has come** (NIV). Have you found that new life in Christ? Have you had a conversion experience? Have you been *vived*? Don't get the cart before the horse. There is no point in pursuing re-*vival* if you have never been *vived*. You can be *vived* here in this moment if you pray this prayer to God from your heart:

> Lord, I know that I am a sinner and that on my own I am not prepared to meet God. I believe that Jesus died to pay the penalty for my sin. I believe that He rose from the dead. Right now in this moment I turn from my sin and I embrace Jesus Christ by faith. Come into my life and forgive my sins. Change me. Make me the man (or woman) You want me to be. I give my life to You today. I pray in Jesus' name. Amen.

This is, by far, the best decision you have ever made. Let someone at your church know about your decision or write letters@walkintheword.com to tell us about your good news.

> *Revival is:*
> *God, gladly at the*
> *center of my life,*
> *experienced and*
> *enjoyed.*

What Revival Is

The word *revive* is used many times in Scripture. Let's look at a few.

Psalm 119:107 says, **I am exceedingly afflicted; *revive* me . . . according to Thy Word** (NASB, emphasis added). Revival involves an increased hunger for and delight in God's Word after a difficult season of life.

Psalm 119:37 instructs, **Turn away my eyes from looking at vanity, and *revive* me in Thy ways** (NASB, emphasis added). Revival involves a disdain for sin and renewed desire for obedience to God.

Psalm 80:18 prompts us to say, ***Revive* us, and we will call upon Thy name** (NASB, emphasis added). Revival brings increased commitment to and interest in personal prayer.

Revival is getting back on the path, getting the goal in view again, and pursuing with new passion the One who can make your life more than you ever dreamed.

Revival is: God, gladly at the center of my life, experienced and enjoyed. I see God working. He's working in my life, and I'm loving it more and more. That's revival.

Maybe you remember a time when you were fired up about the Lord, but somehow you drifted away. Maybe you've become like that guy in the lawn chair at the entrance to our church; you're showing up, but you're missing the mark. Maybe you could say, "Somewhere along the line I lost my passion for the Lord." Well, you *can* have it back, and God *wants* you to have it back! God wants that reviving for each one of us, and there's no biblical reason to doubt it.

This is a book with a specific, intentional plan to take you to a better place with God than you may have ever been before. This is a book about letting God tune your heart strings to the melody you were made to play—a dynamic, delightful, genuine relationship with Him. No matter where you are or what you've done, no matter what you feel or think you need, the clouds of heaven are now bursting with the favor and fullness God would shower upon every place within you that is parched and dry. A deluge of dangerous delight in the God who made you is ready to rain down upon you. This is a book about revival—not in the world, not in our country, not in your church or even in your family, but in *you*. Personal, radical, joyful, biblical revival.

> *I want nothing to be off-limits to God. He can have free access to all that I am, everywhere I go, all the time.*

Promises to Keep

If enjoying a happening relationship with God were easy, everyone would have one. Fact is, most people do not—even those who are really trying. I know that I didn't for a long time. But by God's grace, He's taught me and brought me a long way. More than anything I want to share with you the road I've traveled. I know that you have some questions and wonder how it can happen for you. The answers and some practical activities to fasten what you're learning to your experience are just ahead in these pages.

Before we begin we need to make some promises—promises to ourselves and to God. These promises will keep us going when the road to revival gets rough or steep.

A Promise about Dissatisfaction

**This people honors me with their lips,
but their heart is far from me (Matthew 15:8).**

~ *I promise to be dissatisfied with anything less than
a genuine personal experience with God.* ~

I want more of God in my life. I want more heartfelt worship and more measurable progress in personal righteousness. I don't want to just hear I'm in God's family; I want to *feel* it! I want true joy and peace that penetrates the conceptual and arrives unhindered at the center of a genuine personal experience. I'm tired of routine religion that makes drudgery out of what should be delight. I know that if I keep doing what I've always done, I'm going to keep getting what I have always gotten—and I'm not satisfied with that anymore. I want a real, growing, dynamic relationship with God, and I'm finished settling for less. *I promise.*

Signature _____ Date _____

A Promise about Verification

They received the word with great eagerness, examining the Scriptures daily, to see whether these things were so (Acts 17:11 NASB).

~ *I promise to set God's Word high above human teaching
and to handle it with the respect it deserves.* ~

My goal is not to learn from any human author or pastor or leader—I want to learn from the Lord. I will read the Scripture at the start of each chapter from my own Bible. I will not simply skim the biblical content in search of stories to move me but will carefully read the bold portions where I find them, knowing that I am reading the very words of God. I will reflect upon the truth I read, and whenever possible mark it in my own copy of God's Holy Word. *I promise.*

Signature _____ Date _____

A Promise about Compartmentalization
**The earth is the Lord's, and everything in it
(1 Corinthians 10:26 NIV).**

> ∿ *I promise to give God access
> to every area of my life.* ∿

I will strive not to compartmentalize my faith—by separating out what I can and can't trust God with; as in, "I'll trust Him with my fears, but I can't trust Him with my finances." I promise to make it my unceasing goal to avoid the duplicity of loving God freely in some areas while refusing Him access to other compartments of my life. I want nothing to be off-limits to God. He can have free access to all that I am, everywhere I go, all the time. By God's grace, no compartments. *I promise.*

Signature _____ Date _____

A Promise about Personalization
**First take the log out of your own eye
(Matthew 7:5 NASB).**

> ∿ *I promise to make this a book
> about me and God alone.* ∿

As I read this book, I will focus exclusively on my own relationship with God and my need for personal revival. I will not allow my mind to drift to what others need to learn. Like the oxygen masks on a plane, I will first secure my own mask before I try to be of assistance to others. More than my pastor or my friend or a member of my own family, I freely admit that *I* need a fresh downpour of revival in my life. A total focus on my own need for God, no one else—just me. *I promise.*

Signature _____ Date _____

A Promise about Application
We all have knowledge. Knowledge puffs up
(1 Corinthians 8:1 NKJV).

$\sim$ *I promise to put into practice what I am learning.* $\sim$

I understand that knowledge for its own sake is not enough. I will not stop with merely a mental comprehension of personal revival in my relationship with God, but will put into practice the activities at the end of each chapter. I won't just read some words and agree on a cognitive level, but I will work at applying everything I am learning on a daily basis. *I promise.*

Signature _____ Date _____

Wow—That's a Lot of Promises!

Let me boil it down for you. You're saying this: "I want *more of God* (Promise #1) based on what He's *promised* (Promise #2) to be for me in *every area* (Promise #3) of *my* life (Promise #4), and I will *work at it with my whole heart* (Promise #5). I promise.

Signature _____ Date _____

Without these kinds of commitments undergirding you, you'll just be wasting your time going through this book. You'll read one or two chapters and then go through another disappointing season of mostly duty and hardly any delight in your walk with God. The result would be a further step into shallow, perfunctory spirituality. This information has to get past your head and into your heart or it goes nowhere.

So like I asked, *Are you willing?* In a moment we can pray together a prayer of promise to God. We can tell Him what we are willing to put into this downpour. Rest assured that if we do our part God will do His!

At the end of every chapter, the focus turns inward: *What does this truth mean to me?* These steps are designed to give you a place to begin in offering yourself to God. Plan on investing some personal time with the Lord in these three steps that close each chapter.

ACTIVATE

By the end of each chapter, your head will be full of information. But don't close the book until you move the focus to your heart. In this step, you'll get something to think about, something to do, or some fresh way to make God's truth your own. You will only see real change in your life as you personalize the truth by your actions.

ELEVATE

Need a place to begin with God? Let the written prayers start your conversation with Him . . . and then keep it going on your own. Wait in silence when the words don't come. Pray with expectation, believing that God hears you and that He will respond.

REPLICATE

The Christian life was never meant to be lived solo. God designed His people to mingle together and help one another grow. Make a specific commitment to share in some way with at least one other person what you are learning about personal revival. Don't neglect this critical step! You'll be surprised at the results!

Are you ready to begin? Let's go to God in prayer.

Father, I invite You to do a new work in my heart. I confess that I have been satisfied with less of You than Your Son died to give me. I have been lulled by mediocrity and even believed at times that more of

You was not possible. I have believed the lie that You were unable to help me—but now I believe differently.

Bring a revival to my heart and quench this thirst I have lived with for so long. I hold Your Word in my hands now with expectation. Allow the fresh water of Your Spirit to pour over the dry places in me. Thank You for Your awesome invitation. I begin by faith to move toward You. Thank You for the promise that if I draw near to You, You will draw near to me.

(Continue your prayer with the following.)

Lord, help me to remember that _____

_____

_____

_____.

Teach me to trust You when _____

_____

_____

_____.

Forgive me for _____

_____

_____

_____.

Lord, I remember when our relationship was like _____

_____

_____

_____.

I want that back again. In Jesus' name. Amen.

Come, let us return to the LORD;

for he has torn us, that he may heal us;

he has struck us down, and he will bind us up.

After two days he will revive us;

on the third day he will raise us up,

that we may live before him.

Let us know; let us press on to know the LORD;

his going out is sure as the dawn;

he will come to us as the showers,

as the spring rains that water the earth.

HOSEA 6:1–3

CHAPTER 1

We Need a Downpour

There's something about a dry spell that gets people talking. I've been hearing it from almost everyone: "Man, this has been a dry summer." Yep, there's no denying it, the lack of rain is a big deal. Lawns are dead, fruit stands are deserted, and farmers are defeated. This past summer will go down in the record books as a parched and desolate season, but was it the driest summer we've ever had? Not even close.

If your grandparents are around, they could probably tell you about a drought in the 1930s when it didn't rain for nine years. In the breadbasket of the country, our richest farmlands were turned into a "Dust Bowl." In 1934, thirty-four states experienced severe droughts. On April 14, 1935, a day known as "Black Sunday," the wind whipped across the parched farmland and blew up the dust into an enormous "black blizzard" that whisked away countless acres of topsoil. That's what a drought is like, and most of us have never experienced a real one—not in our countryside at least. But sadly too often we experience a drought in our spirits.

The Bible teaches in Isaiah 58:11 and in many other places that the human heart is like a garden. Your heart is the immaterial part of you that can know God; it's the part that will live forever. If you weed and water and tend your heart as Scripture instructs, you'll experience a bumper crop of God's grace in your life. Conversely, if you fail to garden your heart, first it will become overgrown with weeds, then it will become lifeless and dry, and eventually it will disappear in a dust storm. People who have lost heart are legion.

Does God love us even when our hearts are far from Him? The answer: Yes, He does!

Second Corinthians 4 twice exhorts us not to lose heart because if we do, we've lost everything. No wonder the wisest man who ever lived exhorted, **Guard your heart!** (Proverbs 4:23 NIV). You have to take care of your heart.

Like me, maybe you've experienced some parched days in your relationship with God. Maybe you've known the sadness of falling in exhaustion and watching through weary eyes as your heart for something or someone begins to shrivel. Maybe you've had seasons where time with God was non-existent and weekend worship was "Black Sunday" for sure—not because of where the pastor or the people were in their hearts, but because of where you were in yours. Now hear this: **Times of refreshing may come from the presence of the Lord** (Acts 3:20). The goal of this chapter is that you would begin to believe that.

You—yes, *you*—can have a fresh downpour of God's grace and mercy upon your life. The hands that hold this book can feel a fresh surge of energy to labor for our King. The eyes that see these pages can gaze in renewed wonder and awe upon the God who loves you. The heart that beats within your chest this moment can pulse with renewed joy given by God in response to choices you make and actions you take. Honest! God is not reluctant; He is ready and willing.

Read again this amazing assurance given by the prophet Hosea: **Come, let us return to the LORD; for he has torn us, that** he may heal us; he has struck us down, and he will bind us up. After two days he will revive us; on the third day he will raise us up, that we may live before him. Let us know; let us press on to know the LORD; his going out is sure as the dawn; he will come to us as the showers, as the spring rains that water the earth (Hosea 6:1–3).

How about Some Background?

Of course we can't just rip open God's Word and start reading wherever our eyes happen to fall. You have to know the context of the book, who is speaking for God, and what that particular portion of God's Word is trying to communicate.

Hosea preached for about eighty years. Isaiah and Micah were his contemporaries. Hosea is the first, the largest, and the most theologically complete of the minor prophets. The question answered by Hosea is, *Does God love us even when our hearts are far from Him?* The answer: Yes, He does!

Hosea ministered at a time when the kingdom was divided and the people living in the northern part were called Israel. They were a prosperous people, but they were wayward, idolatrous, and self-indulgent. Sound familiar? They had been successful in their pursuit of what the world offered, and in the process had lost contact with the One they were created to enjoy most—God Himself.

Hosea was called by God to play a unique role for these people. God instructed Hosea to marry a woman named Gomer, who would later become a prostitute. Hosea's faithful love for his unfaithful wife then became a prophetic picture of God's persistent, patient, pursuing love for His obstinate people. Hosea pleaded for a change of heart in order to avoid God's judgment

From the Life of Josiah: We Need a Downpour

2 Kings 22:1–23:27; 2 Chronicles 34–35; Deuteronomy 28:15

The storm clouds had never looked darker over Israel than they did in 640 B.C. Unchecked evil reigned, from the king's palace down to the streets. God's people had not only forgotten Him; now they provoked His anger with their wickedness. God's holy patience had run out. "Enough," He sighed, and started the countdown to judgment.

But to everyone's surprise, out from that dark heritage walked the boy-king Josiah who **did what was right in the eyes of the LORD** (2 Kings 22:2). Standing in the gap between God's holiness and his people's wickedness, young Josiah launched a lifelong crusade to take care of God's business in Israel. His mission was clear: *we're turning back to God*.

Then an amazing thing happened. As Josiah's team rebuilt God's temple, in ruins after generations of neglect, they found God's Book buried in obscurity. At age twenty-six, Josiah read God's Word for the first time, and it took him to his knees.

He hadn't known that God had written down His instructions. He hadn't heard the promises of warning and blessing based on obedience. And now his heart was exposed to God's Word for the first time, and it convicted him to the core.

Josiah realized they were sitting on a time bomb. **Great is the wrath of the LORD that is kindled against us, because our fathers have not obeyed the words of this book** (v. 13). The clock had been ticking all the time God's Word had been buried, and judgment was closer than they realized.

So as a man before God and a king before his nation, Josiah invited God's Word to change their thinking.

- He recognized that some things had to go. *We're going to live differently.*
- He repented of how his nation had walked away from God. *We've been wrong, and we're turning around.*
- He and his people returned to the Lord. *We're leaving this sin behind us. We want what God has for us.*

His mission was again clear: *Revive us, Lord. We need a downpour!*

What happened next changed history. God saw the tenderness and humility of Josiah's heart and had compassion on him and his generation. In His holiness, God could not overlook the evil that had been done, but He held back the clock so that this repentant generation would not experience the consequences.

Revival begins here: with a profound awareness of God's absolute holiness, our absolute sinfulness, and our complete inability to bridge the divide that separates us. Revival always begins with God reaching down to us—not in a trickle of blessing, but in a deluge of Himself that covers our past and welcomes us to begin again.

and to experience the revival that God longed to bring them. God has not changed. What He offered through Hosea then, He offers to you now. *Right now!*

Come Back to Me!

God invites you to come back to Him. No matter how far away you are right now or how long you've been gone, Hosea 6:1 opens the door, **Come, let us return to the LORD,** and then again in verse 3, **Let us know; let us press on to know the LORD.** That's the invitation to revival.

Let's break God's Word down a little more. Notice, **Let us return to the LORD.** Let's turn our lives off our current course and aim all that we are and have where the answers are—with the Lord. Our problems began when we turned away from the Lord, so let's turn back; let's return.

Notice the invitation, "Come." You don't have to be where you are. It's a tenderhearted pleading; you don't have to live the life that you're living. You don't have to experience the sorrow and heartbreak that you're feeling. You can return to the Lord. You can leave where you are and return. It's not too late. God is waiting now with open arms; return to Him!

Doubt can become faith. Discouragement can become joy. Despair can become purpose and fulfillment. Defeat can become victory. "How can that happen in my life?" you ask. I'm telling you how—"return."

Then notice, "Let us." "Us"—as in, "You're not alone." You may feel that you are alone, but you are not. You may wonder if other people care. Believe it—many do, and they want you to experience the joy they have found. Come with us now; we'll go together.

The Hebrew term translated "return" is used more than a thousand times in the Old Testament. It is used more frequently than almost any term describing what God desires for us. It is a picture of repentance. Hosea uses the term twenty-three times. Here's a sampling:

Hosea 5:4: **Their deeds do not permit them to return to their God.** Sometimes our chosen behavior keeps us from returning to the Lord. God is not the barrier; our current deeds are in the way. Keep that in mind.

Hosea 7:10: **The pride of Israel testifies to his face; yet they do not return to the LORD their God, nor seek him.** *Could the problem be my pride?* It's not easy to admit that my heart is parched and dry. It's not easy to confess that what I set off in search of has not delivered what it promised. It's hard to swallow my pride and say that what I really needed is back where I left it, waiting for my return.

Hosea 11:5: **Assyria shall be their king.** A pagan nation was coming to rule over God's people, bringing slavery and bondage **because they have refused to return to me.** Ouch. What if this feeling of being trapped in certain patterns of thinking is simply my refusal to truly return? What if my cyclical failure in certain situations can be traced to my reticence in returning?

Even to the last chapter of his prophetic message, Hosea is still pleading and God is still promising: **I will heal their apostasy; I will love them freely, . . . They shall return and dwell beneath my shadow** (Hosea 14:4, 7). The entire book of Hosea proclaims the assurance that good things await those who *return* to the Lord.

Do You Hear the Alarm?

Returning to the Lord is a decision made at a point in time. Imagine a smoke alarm suddenly going off in the building where you are right now. Instantly you would have a choice to make: remain where you are or get up and move away from the danger. You may not feel that you are in any danger, and so you are slow to respond or you simply ignore the alarm, hoping it will reset itself. Maybe *that is* the danger.

In the same way, maybe you have failed to progress in the countless ways that God has offered to perfect His likeness in your life. If you have grown deaf to that call, returning for you is igniting a fresh passion to follow God with your whole heart.

Returning is a decision made at a particular point in time. Are you ready to make that choice right now? You can read this entire book and gain no benefit if you don't begin by turning to Him. What should you do? Start with understanding what turning really is. It's the following three things.

1. Turning to the Lord Is Recognizing

Think about your life. The call to return to the Lord begins with the recognition that some things have to go. The things that have to go are the ones about which you can say, *This is wrong or harmful to me and those I love. I don't desire this anymore. I recognize it for what it is; I'm returning to the Lord.* You've got to see some things differently. You've got to let God shine His light on your activities inside and out, so that what used to be attractive is recognized for the sin it really is. *No more. I don't want that. The light has gone on; I see it for what it is.* The first part of turning is recognizing that behaviors rigorously rationalized are the real issues in your heart. Puzzled? More help with recognition is ahead. For now, I just want you to understand the concept of seeing in your life what needs to be removed because it's a barrier to the returning you really need.

2. Turning to the Lord Is Repenting

When you see what got you where you are, you don't want it anymore. You are ready for some total honesty. *I'm wrong, God. I'm sorry for what I've done. You deserve better than this. I have no excuse for acting and choosing as I have. I'm unworthy. I'm undeserving, but I'm returning.* Repenting is so important that we are going to spend a whole chapter on it, but know for now that there is no downpour without returning and there is no returning without repentance.

3. Turning to the Lord Is Actually Re-Turning

If you want to experience a downpour of God's mercy, you have to come back to the place where the water flowed before. This is not just an emotional response and a change of your mind; it's also an exertion of your will to get moving again in the right direction. *I'm leaving this sin behind. I don't want this anymore. I don't want the opportunity to sin anymore. I'm not hanging around that temptation; I'm shutting it off and I'm moving away. I'm returning to the Lord. I want what God has for me. First, and most, and best.*

Think of turning to the Lord as discovering a destructive weed in the garden of your heart. First you have to recognize it: "Hey, that's a weed! Get it out of my garden." Then you have to pull it up by the roots—that's repenting—demonstrating that you are really done with that weed. Finally, you have to dispose of the weed so that it cannot sink its roots into your garden again. That's putting some distance between sin and what you want out of your life.

Warning: This Is Not a "Do-It-Yourself" Project

Now, don't try to fix yourself before you return. Don't hear truth like this and say to yourself, "After I get some things sorted out, I'll return. I have to be clean in order to get right with God. I'll take a bath and then I'll return." No, God *is* the bath. Get back to Him. God doesn't need self-reform. He doesn't want our efforts to be apart from Him. He wants just this: for your heart and His to be as close as possible as soon as possible.

Embrace the Need for Crisis

Do you understand the difference between faith in a crisis and faith in the process? Conversion to Christ comes in a crisis. In a certain place at a certain time, you heard the good news about Jesus and by faith you turned from sin and received God's forgiveness. You became a true follower of Jesus at a turning point. That was faith in a crisis.

We are often taught wrongly that once you had that faith in a crisis, then everything else in your Christian life will be a process called sanctification. If you have been taught "process only" sanctification, then the focus of your Christian life becomes being a better dad or mom, learning how to manage your finances, or being a good example at work. And don't forget to show up next Wednesday night for our new study on 2 Samuel or the second coming or something else that starts with "S." This kind of thinking is always adding, adding, adding. More content for a better process. Keep trying, keep growing, keep moving ahead in an endless cycle of data-gathering and hopeful implementation.

Process is important, but process alone will not complete the work God began at your crisis of conversion. Colossians 2:6 says,

As you received Christ Jesus the Lord, so walk in him. I bet if I heard your conversion story it would go something like this:

> I was going along thinking I had it all together, and then God dropped a boulder on my life. He got my attention! I had a problem and realized I couldn't handle it on my own, so I reached out to the Lord; later I realized that it was really God reaching out to me.

> *Returning is more than removing overt sin from our lives. It's a thousand refinements, each of which takes us deeper and further into all that knowing the Lord is.*

Is that pretty much your story? Yeah, it's all of ours. The label on the boulder may be different for each of us (e.g., an existential crisis, a little boy afraid of going to hell, an empty wife in a failing marriage, a normally healthy man with an awful piece of news from the doctor), but the purpose it served was the same. God got our attention. Everyone is converted by faith at a moment of time in some sort of crisis. We thought we had it all together, but we found out we didn't. We needed the Lord, and because of His grace we reached out by faith and found Him.

As you received Christ Jesus the Lord, Paul declares in Colossians 2:6, **so walk in him.** The crises are not supposed to be left in the rearview mirror as we begin to grow in Christ. There needs to be a regular interval of turning and returning to the Lord where the chords of commitment that bind our hearts to His are tightened up again. While we are eternally forgiven the penalty of sin through faith in Christ, the power of that sin still looms large over our old nature. A poor choice, a weak moment, a willful wandering—and we are in need of another crisis.

Don't just try harder; return to the Lord. Not because He has left you (He hasn't!) but because, like Jonah, in some way, at some level, you have left Him. As you received Him (a moment of turning) so walk in Him (a moment of *returning*). Every so often as we follow Christ through the months and years, we need to say, "I have slipped. How did I get over here? I must return to the Lord."

The Need for Crisis = Nothing New

For two thousand years the church has understood the need for regular *returning* or *reviving*. I have a three-inch-thick book on my shelf entitled *Accounts of Revival* that is filled with stories of revival in the lives of countless people through the centuries. It was published in 1754, then revised in 1845. But for the past 150 years, there has been less and less emphasis on reviving in the experience of a believer—only the crisis of conversion followed by an endless process that leads most people to a spiritual drought, desperately in need of a downpour.

Take it from me, if you've known Christ for three or four years, you probably need another crisis. Possibly you believe that your life is just fine as it is. Returning is more than removing overt sin from our lives. It's a thousand refinements, each of which takes us deeper and further into all that knowing the Lord is.

Where's My Church in All This?

The Church of the Brethren, a fairly typical evangelical denomination, honestly self analyzed:

Most Church of the Brethren congregations no longer plan for revivals. That is not because they do not need them, it is the lack of interest, the lack of attendance and support for them in general that has brought about their demise. As Bible interest has waned in the Church of the

Brethren, so have our membership numbers, and our
worship attendance and our giving. At the same time our
leadership needs have increased. Our marriage break-
ups have multiplied, youth in our culture has become
a bigger and bigger issue. We're losing our children. It's
also true that at the time when many congregations have
reduced their interest in revival an interest and attention
have grown to church sports leagues. This in itself is a sad
commentary on the current state in the church."*

Even fifty years ago in Baptist and Methodist and most other
Protestant denominations, churches would hold a special series
of revival meetings every eighteen months to two years in order
to provoke this crisis of returning. The pastor would announce,
"We're going to have some revival meetings." A week would be
set aside, and a guest preacher would bring an urgent and more
crisis-oriented message than the people got week in and week out.
These revival preachers moved from church to church and focused
their entire ministry on these weeks of "returning to the Lord." In
effect their message was, "What are you doing way over there?"
and the people would agree, "You're right. I don't even want to be
over here; thanks for reminding me where I really want to be. I'm
coming back right now."

That pattern is almost gone from the churches of our day. Our
"special speakers" actually take us deeper and more analytically
into our process. We are offered endless teaching and tapes, books,
and seminars on "how-to's." How to be a better friend/neighbor/
witness, how to communicate with your spouse, how to make a
difference at work, how to make peace with your past, etc. So much
of the teaching today is about horizontal behavioral adjustments,

---

*www.brfwitness.org/Articles/2001v36n3.htm

Jonathan Edwards and the First Great Awakening (1734)

If you asked anyone living in the early 1730s in the original thirteen American colonies to direct you to a church on fire for God, they would have shrugged their shoulders and shook their heads. People's hearts were far from God—even in the churches.

In 1733, Jonathan Edwards was pastor of the Congregational Church in Northampton, Massachusetts. According to Edwards, it was a "degenerate time" in his city, marked by a "dullness of religion." "The young people were addicted to night walking, tavern drinking, lewd practices among the sexes the greater part of the night. Family government did too much fail in the town." For years, the town had been sharply divided between two feuding parties who jealously opposed one another in all public affairs. Edwards prayed fervently for individuals to turn back to God.

And God was preparing the field. In a nearby village, two young people died suddenly in the spring of 1734. The town was jarred into thinking about their eternal destinies. People began to seek God. That fall, Edwards preached on justification by faith alone, and six people received Christ as their Savior. One of them was a young woman who was "one of the greatest company keepers [probably a prostitute] in the whole town." Her life was so radically changed that everyone could tell it was a work of God's grace. Over the next six months, three hundred people were "hopefully converted" in this town of eleven hundred.* Edwards said:

> God seemed to have gone out of His usual way in the quickness of His work, and the swift progress His Spirit has made in His operation on the hearts of many . . . . There was scarcely a single person in the town, either old or young, that was left unconcerned about the great things of the eternal world . . . . The town seemed to be full of the presence of God: it never was so full of love, nor so full of joy . . . . Our public assemblies were then beautiful; the congregation was alive in God's service, every one earnestly intent on the public worship . . . . Our public praises were then greatly enlivened; God was then served . . . in the beauty of holiness.†

It was this revival, and Edwards' reporting of it, that provoked people on both sides of the Atlantic to seek God for a downpour of mercy in their lives. They were not disappointed. Under the leadership of men like Jonathan Edwards, George Whitefield, and John Wesley, the church grew very rapidly in New England between 1740 and 1742 with more than three hundred thousand new and revived Christians turning to the Lord in faith and repentance. One historian called this time, "The most glorious and extensive revival our country has ever known."

---

*Henry Blackaby and Claude King, *Fresh Encounter* (Nashville: LifeWay Press, 1996), 42.
†Adapted from Jonathan Edwards, "Narrative of Surprising Conversions," in *The Works of President Edwards* (New York: Leavitt & Allen, 1857), 231–72, as quoted by Blackaby and King, 42.

but there is very little on the vertical focus of you and God. The sad result, as every survey confirms, is very little heart transformation. We used to believe that if we got our lives where they needed to be with the Lord, the other stuff would fall in place.

What we desperately need is a crisis, a turning, a returning to the Lord. There will be no revival without it. Not under any circumstances.

Stop Here for an Honest Question

When was the last time you had a spiritual crisis in your life? When was the last time God brought you to your knees with the weight of weeds growing unwanted and treacherous in the garden of your heart? When did you last have a deep, heartfelt rekindling of love and passion for God's Word? How recently has your heart been so tender that you wept over lost people in your family or your coworkers who desperately need the Savior, and who are in danger of hell if they were to die today? If your honest answer is like most believers I know, respond now to the invitation: **Come, let us return to the Lord.**

And What If I Do?

Are you uncertain about how a revived heart will feel? Maybe you wonder if you have ever really experienced one. Do you fear deep down that a downpour of God's mercy might overwhelm your faith? Hosea wants to make sure we know what to expect, so he quantifies our returning in terms of a precise goal. **Let us know; let us press on to know the Lord.**

The "knowledge of the Lord" is a frequent and fascinating phrase in Scripture. Its first usage is in Exodus 5:2 where Pharaoh said, **I do not know the** LORD. In Isaiah 11:9 the prophet predicts that in the final days of human history, **the earth shall be full of the knowledge of the** LORD **as the waters cover the sea.** How great will that be? The knowledge of the Lord—to the rooftops. Phenomenal!

If you were to study every occurrence of "the knowledge of the Lord" in Scripture, you would see four distinct aspects that fill out our understanding of how awesome this knowledge of the Lord really is.

1. Knowledge of the Lord Consists of Facts about God

Oh, the depth of the riches both of the wisdom and knowledge of God (Romans 11:33 NASB). It's the infinite information about God. It's who He is and what He's done; it's God's resume. How much do you know about the Lord? Can you list ten of God's most awesome attributes and show where they are revealed in Scripture? Information is powerful, but information is not an end in itself.

2. Knowledge of the Lord Is a Heart Understanding of Those Facts

I know people who have half the Bible memorized, but it doesn't download into their lives. They are walking around spouting what they know while their hearts are filled with hatred or hypocrisy. Having facts about God is clearly not enough. You've got to have heart understanding of the facts. It's not just information—it's inspiration. Facts are good, of course. Jesus said, **"Love . . . . God . . . with all your mind,"** but also with your heart and soul and strength (Matthew 22:37; Mark 12:30; Luke 10:27).

God wants us to *feel* the facts we know about Him. I want to feel it, too! I want to be touched at the core of my being. I don't want to just know stuff *about* God; I want to sense the reality of my eternal relationship *with* Him. Facts, then feelings, and even that's not all. . . .

3. Knowledge of the Lord Is an Experience with God

Paul said in Acts 17:28, **In him we live and move and have our being.** Everywhere I go, God is there. God is with me at work and in my car and at my computer. I can experience the Lord's presence when I meet someone at the grocery store, over the back fence, or in the emergency room. Do you have that continual sense of God's presence? Has that sense of His presence been growing or fading in your life? You can have it back if you don't have it now. It is all part of the knowledge of the Lord. Facts and feelings and experience with God.

4. Knowledge of the Lord Is Blessing from God

James 1:17 says, **Every good and perfect gift is from above** (NIV). Part of the knowledge of the Lord is an awareness that everything I have is from God. Here I am today with life and breath and health and strength. The knowledge of the Lord is being aware of what an immense grace those basic things are. The day may come when we look back at this time in our lives and say that these were the greatest times we ever knew. But here in this moment, we want to connect the blessings that flow our way as truly undeserved gifts from God. I don't have the right to draw another breath, but here I am under the clouds of mercy. Like a little child laughing in the rain and running to catch the drops with his tongue, I am delighting in the God who gives such perfect gifts.

When Hosea says, **Let us press on to know the LORD,** he is talking about these four ways we can have knowledge of the Lord. I am sure there is also much more the Lord will yet reveal to us. When we talk of personal revival, we envision a passionate pursuit of the knowledge of the Lord.

Notice how the words "press on" call for our enthusiastic effort. The original language actually implies, "Let us know . . . stop . . . hold the phone, everybody freeze, no passive knowing allowed, 'let us *press on* to know'" (emphasis added). It's like he stops midsentence and says, "Let us know—wait, we need more than everyday energy in the matter of knowing eternal God. Let us *press on* to know."

> *I want every detail of every circumstance of every moment of every day to awaken my heart to the reality of God and His nearness. I want to see and sense and savor the nearness of God in all things.*

The phrase "press on" is a military term that can be translated as "persecute." It describes the way a victorious warrior conquered, then vanquished his foe. It's intentionality and intensity all rolled into one. *I'm going after this myself.* I'm not going to just sit back and let my pastor stick a funnel in my ear and fill me up with the knowledge of the Lord. *I'm* going after it! *I'm* going to pursue it! *I'm* going to put some intensity into this!

Let us pursue the knowledge of the Lord. Let's give ourselves to this.

It's intense. It takes effort. It takes energy. It takes enthusiasm. So often as a pastor, I want to say to people, "Man, quit being so passive. Don't be so lazy and sluggish about your faith. This is worth more than you're giving it. Quit letting your spiritual life come to you; get fired up about it." Pressing on to know the Lord means waking up and giving that pursuit everything you have.

Romans 13:11 says that it's **high time to awake out of sleep** (NKJV). Wake up and pursue the Lord. God's invitation goes out to all of us to wake up and give our relationship with Him all that it deserves.

Can I Have Your Attention?

I got a wake-up call recently. I was driving out to our Elgin church campus where there is a lot of construction going on. About ten trucks hauling steel arrive at the church each day, delivering materials for our new worship center. I was in the right-hand turn lane into the campus driveway with one of those steel trucks in line ahead of me. The trailer was loaded with two enormous "I" beams that will span the roof of the worship center. Talking to one of my brothers on my cell phone, I said, "Hey, this is kind of weird. It looks like this truck in front of me is backing up." About a second later I realized it *was* backing up! I tried to slam the car in reverse but BAM!—the whole windshield exploded with the force of those two girders coming right at me. Over the dashboard and into the car they came and then suddenly stopped . . . just short of my head. I don't know what would have happened if the driver hadn't stopped.

The driver felt bad about the accident. When he found out I was the church's pastor, he felt even worse. He was a young believer and was so excited to be helping to build a church. I imagined him going home and telling his wife, "Well, honey, my day was kind of mixed. I had the joy of delivering materials that will help build a church, but I almost killed the pastor." It was a close call. I asked him, "Why did you stop?" He said, "I felt something." Sure he did—through multiple tons of steel, he felt my windshield breaking. God was giving me a little wake-up call.

We don't know how long we have on this earth, do we? Here's what this episode reminded me of: I want every detail of every circumstance of every moment of every day to awaken my heart to the reality of God and His nearness. I want to see and sense and savor the nearness of God in all things. **Let us press on to know the LORD.** It's a picture of urgency.

Maybe like me you wonder, *How many more days am I going to get in this world? Really, how much time do I have? I am not ready to meet the Lord yet.* Spiritually, in Jesus, I believe that I am prepared by God's grace to meet Him, but I'm not satisfied by what has been accomplished yet. I'm not satisfied with the heights and the depths and the places that I've been to in my own relationship with the Lord. I want more time to go further, to go higher, to go deeper. I want to make good use of the time that remains for me and to respond to this amazing invitation.

> *That circumstance . . . that situation you would plead with God to change, that thing you hate that He allowed because He loves you—will you let Him call your heart back and more deeply into Him?*

The invitation is to personal revival. Let's turn to the Lord. Let's *return* to the Lord.

You say, "James, I want to do that. How do I get more of that in my life?" Well, notice the mysterious path that Hosea describes which leads us to more of the Lord.

Through Pain to Purpose

Looking again at our Hosea 6:1 passage, we read an intriguing phrase, **[God] has torn us, that he may heal us.** The word *torn* is used of a predator that grabs its prey, shreds it with its sharp teeth, then consumes it. It's the word that Jacob spoke when his murderous sons brought back their brother's coat of many colors. Jacob

said, **Joseph has surely been torn to pieces** (Genesis 37:33 NIV).
It's a severe word and kind of unsettling to see it describing God's
work in us.

Come, let us return to the LORD; **for he has torn us.** The
Hebrew language is very explicit, "*He* is the one. It is God who has
done this." Make no mistake! God is behind the hurt in your life.
When your life feels torn in two, God has not abandoned you. Far
from moving away in callousness, He is moving toward you with
compassion for the pain He has allowed. He is totally committed
to you as He accomplishes the purposes for that pain.

Why does God do that? Why does God approve pain's intru-
sion into our personal experience? God is trying to bring about
another crisis. Like an electron magnet, God is drawing your heart
back to His. Whatever the particular point of pain is, the circumstance you would most change, the unwanted source of shock and
sadness that you beg God to reverse or resolve . . . God has a purpose for that pain. And it will not go away until the reason for its
arrival has been completed in you. Worse, when God has finished
His work in that part of your life, He will move on to another area
He wants to change in you. God is relentless in His pursuit of us.
His love is not a pampering love; it's a perfecting love. The pathway to revival is through pain. God calls you back through pain,
further and deeper into Him.

One Man Who Had Another Crisis

Recently I spoke with a man in our church named Tim. He told
me that though he had Christian parents and grandparents, and
even though he knew the gospel well and trusted Christ at an early
age, he wandered far from God while in high school. As an adult,
he attended church, but his heart was very far from the Lord.

His stubborn rebellion and refusal of God's will cost him his first marriage. He reported that drugs, alcohol, and sexual sin in their ugliest forms were controlling his life. Even before Tim told me, I knew what God would do about this prodigal son. Our Father God came after him.

Through pain to purpose, God tugged at Tim's heart, first through divorce and the death of a dear friend. Even in this, Tim fought and stubbornly refused God's loving invitation to return, so God showed up at work.

> *God knows you're in the fire. His hand is on the thermostat, and He knows exactly how hot things are getting at your house. He is waiting very carefully for the appointed time.*

Tim installs petroleum tanks at gas stations. One day while he was sizing up a job, a tow truck came around the corner. The driver didn't see him; and before he could get out of the way, the truck struck him down.

"First I felt the front wheels," Tim says, "then I felt my pelvis cracking, breaking in four places." He tried to crawl out from under the truck before the back wheels went over him, but he couldn't move fast enough.

He could have died; he should have died; but the Lord didn't let him die. Into intensive care Tim went with multiple surgeries and a month of painful crisis ahead.

Through pain to purpose. Tim reports that even through this, he was still fighting for his way over God's, still slapping and spurning the hand of grace. Tim told me that it was only when his second wife gave him the "something's going to change" speech that he finally gave in to God. Only when Tim faced losing his second marriage and children through his own rebellion did he let God get hold of his life. He began listening to www.walkintheword.com, our radio ministry, and attending our church. There, under the conviction of the Holy Spirit, Tim got his life and family back on track with God.

The Lord brought Tim to a crisis, a turning point. God's Spirit brought Tim to a post-conversion crisis, a returning to the Lord.

Will you let life's pain bring you to God's purposes?

He was recently baptized at our church. Before he went under the water and came up committed to new life in Christ, he said through his tears, "I'm just so thankful to God that He called me back. I can't believe He loves me so much that He'd want me back." Check out his baptism at www.downpour.org.

You have to come to that place of crisis again and again. If you've known the Lord for a decade, you still need that returning—maybe even more so. God forgive us for trying to live the Christian life as all process and no crisis.

I am so thankful to God that you are reading this message for your heart. Right now, the invitation is going out to you. Is He calling you back? If yes, there is going to be some recognizing, there's going to be some repenting, and there's going to be some returning to the Lord. Look up by faith. The clouds of heaven are bursting with the grace that God wants to shower upon you.

God wants to accomplish His purpose in your pain. Is your marriage struggling? That's God working there. Your difficult work environment, your stubborn child, your sickness in body or soul—it's the Lord calling you back to Him, or more deeply into the love relationship with the Lord that you've built with Him through the years.

The closing verses of Hosea 5 give context to this call to return: **For I [God] will be like a lion to [Israel] . . . I, even I, will tear**

**and go away; I will carry off, and no one shall rescue . . . until
they acknowledge their guilt and seek my face, and in their distress earnestly seek me** (Hosea 5:14–15).

God wants my heart closer to His so He comes like a lion
through some painful circumstances. Then He waits until I respond
to it by acknowledging where I need to change and begin to earnestly seek Him. Is God waiting on you this moment? Can you see
the Great Lion off to the side waiting right now with your "flesh"
between His teeth?

C. S. Lewis touches on this theme in his Narnia Chronicles.
Before the children meet Aslan, they hear about how he ravaged
the enemy.

> "Ooh! Is he quite safe? I shall be nervous about meet-
> ing a lion," Lucy asked.
> "That you will be, dearie. . . . If there's anyone who can
> appear before Aslan without their knees knocking, they're
> either braver than most or else just silly."
> "Then he isn't safe?" said Lucy.
> "Safe?" Said Mr. Beaver: "Who said anything about
> safe? 'Course he isn't safe. But he's good."

By faith, can you see Him there—the Lion of Judah? That circumstance that He is working for your good (Romans 8:28), that
situation you would plead with God to change, that thing you hate
that He allowed because He loves you—will you let Him call your
heart back and more deeply into Him?

Through pain to purpose. That's what the goal is: **He has torn
us, that he may heal us.** Truth be told, we want the healing without the tearing. If that were possible, God would want it too. God
wants to heal your finances, God wants to heal your failure, God

wants to heal your family. But if pain won't get you to return to the Lord, God will press His point further.

Through Death to Life

Hosea 6:1 concludes, **He has struck us down.** The word translated "struck down" has meaning on several levels. It can mean a slap, like to an animal's hindquarters, "Giddyup. Let's go." It can also mean an extended beating to bring submission to the will of the one who is striking down.

The goal of course is that God would bind us up: **He has struck us down, and he will bind us up.** Please don't judge God harshly. He is the lion that tears, but only so He can heal. He is the one who strikes down, but only so He can bind us up. God's goal is always that the pain He brings would take us to a better place. Surgeons don't lament the pain of their procedure. Just as a physician must wound to heal, just as bones are purposely broken to be properly set, just as the skin must be cut to remove a tumor, or the sternum must be sawn in two to repair the heart, so God inflicts pain to ensure that our hearts will make their way finally to the only fountain of true joy—God Himself.

God's role in our suffering is for our good. Job says, **Despise not the discipline of the Almighty. For he wounds, but he binds up; he shatters, but his hands heal** (Job 5:17–18).

And If I Don't Return?

God would rather see you anywhere else than living in rebellion and resistance to His will. Once you come to the cross of Christ, God's will for you is your sanctification (1 Thessalonians 4:3). If you're not advancing in that process, God will take you to some awful places so that His purposes in you might be accomplished.

I'm thinking right now of a couple who attended our church for many years. I remember a conversation with the wife one Sunday after service. She was sobbing, with her small children by her side, standing in an aisle near the front of our worship center. Her sad story is tragically too common. To the shock of everyone who knew them, her gifted husband had traded in his wife, his children, his career, his reputation, his ministry—everything—for someone else who he thought could give him something more.

> *You can be on your way to a better place with God than you've been in a long time by the end of today if you will turn and return to God on His terms.*

Well, he has a lot less now. As I often say, "Choose to sin, choose to suffer." I asked his broken wife, "What's it going to take for God to get his attention?" She said, "He may have to go to ruins." I had never heard that phrase before, so I looked it up.

Nobody wants to "go to ruins." Hosea's phrase, **He has struck us down,** can also mean death. That's what "ruins" is. Sometimes God brings us to death or a state where death would be easier. Call it absolute rock bottom; call it ruins.

God would rather see us anywhere else than running from Him. God would rather see us in a hospital bed than living in rebellion against Him. God would rather see us broken and bankrupt than for Him not to be the **pearl of great price** (Matthew 13:46 NKJV) to us. God would rather see us in a world of hurt than not be the prize of our highest affections. God is willing to do whatever it takes to bring us to that level of relationship.

Some Good News!

The pain that God allows is for a specified period of time. It is for a specific duration, and it most definitely will not go on

forever. Verse 2 says, **After two days he will revive us; on the
third day he will raise us up.** That's not a reference to Easter or
the resurrection of Christ. It's not about Jesus' resurrection; it's
about yours and mine. God brings us low, even to the point of
death, in order to bring us up again.

The point of the reference to two days and a third is that suffering in the life of a believer is for a specified period of time. God
knows you're in the fire. His hand is on the thermostat, and He
knows exactly how hot things are getting at your house. He is waiting very carefully for the appointed time. The moment you go from
denying to acknowledging, the moment you move from seeking
elsewhere to seeking Him, God will turn down the heat. You've
got to know He will. Suffering is appointed for two or three days, a
very specific amount of time and not a moment longer.

God loves you and will not allow you to be **tempted beyond
what you are able** (1 Corinthians 10:13 NASB). Job confirms that life's
pain is for a defined duration: **But He knows the way I take; when
He has tried me, I shall come forth as gold** (Job 23:10 NASB).

Will you let life's pain bring you to God's purposes? Or will
you have to go to ruins? Will God have to tear that sin—that self-
indulgence, that silly, sordid something—out of your life? Will
God have to rip it from your cold, lifeless hands? I plead with you
not to wait that long. Turn now. Acknowledge what God is trying
to teach you, and return to the Lord. Begin to earnestly seek Him,
and you will experience a reviving of your own heart that will be
beyond what you have even imagined.

The Experience of Personal Revival

Hosea concludes 6:3 with two promising phrases about the
experience of revival. Here's the first one: **His going out is sure**

as the dawn. "Going out" is a military term for an army's troops marching out to battle. Every morning the sun comes up, and God goes out to work in the world. Every day the sun comes up, and God continues His work all around you. This revival that we're talking about?— you can have it. Nothing is in the way— only you.

> *When revival comes to the human heart, it's not some gentle, summer, sunshine rain. It's not a sprinkle here and there or a scattered shower. When revival comes to the human heart, it's a torrent, it's a cascade, it's a deluge. It's a downpour!*

Maybe you feel as though these heights of spiritual experience are for others but not for you. Maybe you have felt alone on the sidelines watching others delight themselves in the Lord and wondering why you seem to be missing out. It's not because of God. He is not reluctant to give to you. He never thinks or feels, "You're getting to be a big hassle. Why do you always want more?" God's supply is limitless. God is also not capricious. He's not like, "*You* can be revived but not you over there and, sorry, nothing at all for you guys. But oh, I really like her; she can have everything she wants." God's not like that; He loves all of us equally. There are no second-class citizens or favorites in God's family.

A revived heart is abundantly available for everyone, every day, just as surely as the sun came up this morning. God is doing the work. Hosea 6 constantly affirms that: **He may heal us . . . he will bind us up . . . his going out . . . he will come to us.** Who's doing all this? God is, without reluctance or capriciousness, and He lovingly makes a revived heart available to every one of His children, every day of their lives.

Listen, you can't bring revival to your nation, you can't assure revival in your church or even in your own home. But you can experience it in your heart. You can be on your way to a better place with God than you've been in a long time by the end of today, if you will turn and return to God on His terms.

Concerning God, Make No Small Plans

What God gives, He gives in abundance. He would never respond to your parched heart with, "Oh, here's a tiny bit. See if that will satisfy you. This is all I can give right now, but come back later if you want a wee bit more." Does God give like that? No, God gives like this: **Pressed down, shaken together, running over** (Luke 6:38), **exceedingly abundantly above all that we ask or think** (Ephesians 3:20 NKJV).

To make that abundance abundantly clear, Hosea uses the analogy of rain in the nation of Israel: **He will come to us as the showers.** When revival comes to the human heart, it's not some gentle, summer, sunshine rain. It's not a sprinkle here and there or a scattered shower. When revival comes to the human heart, it's a torrent, it's a cascade, it's a deluge. It's a downpour!

The rainfall in Israel is very infrequent except in the spring and the fall. In those seasons it is very heavy. The term *showers* refers to the darting rain, the heavy, violent mid-October through mid-December downpour. The *spring rains* come in the latter half of February through April. This rain is the intense, saturating, much-anticipated drenching that nourishes the crops and readies the harvest. Bottom line: God will come to us in abundance. **He will come to us . . . as the spring rains that water the earth.**

My Downpour and My Vision for Yours

Three years ago I was going through a very difficult time in my life and ministry. Our church was growing beyond our ability to park and seat people. We packed crowds into four services, with six shuttle busses running, and no solution in sight. I had been praying and fasting for a particular piece of property and had become far too attached to what I was convinced God was going to do for us. I came perilously close to demanding my way from God and calling it faith. I was on the very edge of an experience like the children of Israel had when they got way too pushy with God. **And He gave them their request, but sent leanness into their soul** (Psalm 106:15 NKJV). In my book *Gripped by the Greatness of God*, I tell the story of God's miraculous provision for our church family and the miracle we experienced together, but maybe the bigger miracle was the reviving that took place in my own life.

I had been thinking that I needed a particular answer to prayer. I had pleaded and prodded and pushed my opinion with God to the point where it became idolatry. God wants us to want Him and to believe that He is enough. God desires us to desire Him above all else. When He got my attention, I realized how consumed I had become with this request and how far I had moved from seeking only Him. More than anything I needed revival. I needed God to lift my eyes from the pain I was experiencing and create contentment in my circumstance. Satisfaction in Him and Him alone.

During this time I began to study and pray and sometimes fast about the subject of personal revival, asking God to do it with me. Then one night I had a very special dream. I hesitate to share it lest you think I am being presumptuous. I do not claim that the dream was a revelation or even that God was directly involved, only that He has greatly used it. Nothing like this had happened to me before, nor has anything like it happened since.

Let Me Tell You about My Dream

In my dream, God was working in my life, our church, and our country in an awesome, unparalleled way. Like a mighty river overflowing its banks, God's Spirit was washing across our nation, bringing repentance and revival in a way that has not been seen for centuries. In my dream, I remember knowing without a doubt that it was the Lord's doing, and it was **marvelous in [my] eyes** (Psalm 118:23). Every willing heart was caught up in a heaving sea of grace and love that was God Himself. I felt a joy and peace that eclipses any human experience I have ever known. It was just a taste of something that obliterated anything I had ever called satisfaction.

In my dream, I stood stunned and silent as gentle tears of rejoicing ran down my cheeks. Then I awoke to a pillow wet with tears. I quickly slipped out of bed to collect in my memory all that I had dreamt. I can only say this: What I felt and observed was so moving and so strongly my heart's desire that my consuming passion ever since has been to live in a day when God moves like that.

As I stood in the darkness and soaked in what I had seen, an outline came into my mind. Faster than you can read the rest of this chapter, five things came forcefully to my thinking, and I have not altered a single word to this day. In fact I prayed about these five things for a whole year before I even told the elders of our church. These five points have been the subjects of my preaching and the continuous thoughts of my heart from that day to this. Together they form the remainder of this book and I believe a biblical pathway to personal revival. These five subjects are the way to get under the downpour that God is ready to shower upon your life.

1. God on the Throne: A Picture of Holiness
2. Sin in the Mirror: A Picture of Brokenness
3. Self in the Dirt: A Picture of Repentance
4. Christ on the Cross: A Picture of Grace
5. Spirit in Control: A Picture of Power

Those are the five things I want to study with you from God's Word throughout the rest of these pages. They are, I believe, the pathway to personal revival. I want to lead you and travel that road with you, but first there must be that crisis of returning. Take some time now and come to that crisis with the Lord.

ACTIVATE

1. Draw a spiritual lifeline. Where are you, and where have you been in your spiritual journey? On a blank piece of paper, draw a horizontal line across the length of the paper.

2. Label the left point with your birth date and draw a vertical line at every five-year increment to the present, and label those markers with the year.

3. Draw a bold dot on your lifeline for every significant event in your life (salvation, graduations, wedding dates, birth/death of loved ones, career milestones, relocations, etc.). Label them with a short description.

4. Draw another bold dot above or below the line describing the "mountain tops" or "valleys" in your spiritual life and write above it what your relationship with God was like during that time. When did God show up? When did you not see His hand? When was your relationship satisfying or stale?

5. Write somewhere on the page, "Lord, bring a downpour to my life." Describe in as many words as it takes what you would

like God to do in your life. Place an "X" on the timeline, marking today. Write above it, "Start here."

6. As you review your life, commit this desire to the Lord, "From this day forward, God . . . ."

ELEVATE

Lord, I'm choosing today as my crisis. I am turning around. I am pressing on to know You. Take me to a new level of belonging to You. Reign over me like I've never known before.

Lord, nothing is off-limits to You. Go anywhere in my life and say anything to me. No place of sinfulness, no place of defeat, or selfishness or self-indulgence is hidden from You. All that I am and have, it's Yours.

I'm weary of being dry and passionless. See the true condition of my heart. Thank you for the assurances of Your grace as I am now responding to Your awesome invitation.

Immerse me in a mighty work of Your Spirit that eclipses everything I've experienced to date. Start today, Lord. I need a downpour.

Start today, Lord, by _____

_____

_____

_____.

In Jesus' name. Amen.

REPLICATE

Remembering the Joy of Your Salvation

What was your life like before you came to Christ? One woman said on her one-year spiritual birthday, "I don't know how I lived before. I was so empty . . . and now I am so full."

We're focusing in this study on personal revival—a bringing back to life after indifference or decline. No matter how long it's been since you've come to Jesus as your Savior, think back to the joy of your salvation.

Want to really fire up your passion for God? Get together a small group of believers (preferably of your same gender) and agree that over a meal or coffee time you will share with one another the story of how you came to Christ for salvation. Though you may or may not have a "dramatic testimony," remember that every transformed life is a miracle. Keep your time focused on your point of crisis as the prompting for your initial decision to trust Christ. Discuss together the changes in your life since that time.

You may also want to take this opportunity to share your desire for personal revival and what you've learned in this first chapter. The effort to express your vision for personal revival has great benefit—to you and to others!

In the year that King Uzziah died

I saw the Lord sitting upon a throne, high and lifted up;

and the train of his robe filled the temple. Above him stood

the seraphim. Each had six wings: with two he covered his

face, and with two he covered his feet, and with two he flew.

And one called to another and said:

"Holy, holy, holy is the LORD *of hosts;*

the whole earth is full of his glory!"

And the foundations of the thresholds shook at the voice of

him who called, and the house was filled with smoke.

ISAIAH 6:1–4

CHAPTER 2

God on the Throne: A Picture of Holiness

There can be no personal revival without a right view of God. If you want more of God in your life, begin with "more accurate." What comes to your mind when you think about God? What do you picture when you consider deity? Not what do you think He looks like, but how do you envision God's capacities and interests? What do you believe matters to Him, and where do you conclude His great interests and passions reside?

A. W. Tozer rightly observed that what you think about God is the most important thing about you. It's true whether you realize it or not: your entire life revolves around your view of God. Your personal spiritual revival is waiting. The downpour begins with an exalted view of God.

The Bible repeatedly reveals that the God of the universe resides in a throne room; He is there right now. In this chapter we will look at the major throne-room scenes in Scripture. Through the centuries, God in His grace has allowed certain messengers to visit His throne room, and we are going to see it afresh through their eyes.

Before we begin, let's get a definition on the table that will serve us well on our tour. The single word that summarizes God, His presence, and His throne room—all things that relate to God—is the word *holiness*.

What Exactly Is Holiness?

The Hebrew term is *qodesh*, the Greek is *hagios*. Both mean "to be set apart." When we say *holiness*, we mean God is not like us at all, not in any way. He's different. We would say "awesome" or "unbelievable" or "unfathomable." That's holiness. God is more righteous and pure, more piercing and powerful, more strong and impenetrable than anything we can imagine. We comprehend only fractionally, even infinitesimally, all that He is. He's so different—so *other*—so holy. Every time you hear the word *holy*, think separation; God is completely apart and entirely different than you and me.

If we're going to see revival in our own lives, it has to start here: a right view of the infinitely exalted nature of God Himself. All revival flows from this fountain: a biblical view of God Himself.

I Don't Want That!

At the core of our sinfulness is our desire to usurp God. Can you admit that? Because of our ancestry in the Garden of Eden, we were born with the desire to gain the position that belongs to God and God alone. In Genesis 3, Adam and Eve listened to the lie that they could be like God because they craved what belongs to God alone. In Genesis 11, man again sets out on a foolish plan to make a name for himself by building a tower **with its top in**

the heavens. In Romans 1 we learn of the propensity of every human heart to exchange God's truth for a lie and to worship the creature rather than the Creator. Yes, in all of us is a self-centered bent to get me up and to get God down. There will be no downpour until that sinful inclination is reversed.

> *Every time you hear the word* holy, *think separation; God is completely apart and entirely different than you and me.*

At the core of our being is the desire to reduce this thing called holiness so that there's seemingly no separation between us and God. When God is humanized and man is deified, holiness is lost. Everything gets out of perspective. The first step in personal revival is to get God in His rightful place.

When God is recognized as being above me, beyond me, highly exalted, over me, and totally separate from me, I am getting in position for a downpour. When I embrace God for who He is and I understand who I am—when I know God's place, I can know my place—then things start to fall into place. That's what God's holiness does for us—it puts everything and everyone in their rightful place.

Isaiah 6 is the hub for our study on holiness. It's the place where Isaiah saw the throne room of heaven and was captured by four insights into God's holiness. Each observation will then be confirmed and expanded through our study of another scriptural visitor to that same throne room. See for yourself what Isaiah

God = Where Holiness Meets Love

We have been conditioned by a hyper-grace environment to overestimate God's love and forbearance and to underestimate God's justice, vengeance, and holiness. But it is God's holiness that is the core of His being. If it were love, God would just welcome us all into heaven and say, "Oh, come on in; we'll work out that sin stuff later." That is not what He said. Holiness first demanded that sin be paid for, and only then did love find a way.

saw, and under the direction of God's Spirit, what he wrote for us in God's Word.

Holiness Describes Separation

In the year that King Uzziah died (Isaiah 6:1). King Uzziah reigned fifty-two years in the nation of Israel. Imagine the shock waves that would course through our nation if we lost a ruler who had led us for fifty-two years. Uzziah was the only king most of the people had ever known. When he died, people were in an uproar, wondering who would rule next and what would become of the nation as they had known it. The people were filled with perplexity, fear, and uncertainty.

Heavenly Throne Room Scene #1

It was that year, 740 B.C., when Isaiah **saw the Lord.** We're not told whether Isaiah was waking or sleeping, in a vision or in a dream, only that he was supernaturally transported to the throne room of the God of the universe. The first words from his mouth in this report of his heavenly visit were, **I saw the Lord.** John 12:41 tells us that it was actually the pre-incarnate Christ that Isaiah gazed upon in Isaiah 6. **No one has seen God,** John 1:18 says and continues with, **The only begotten Son, who is in the bosom of the Father, He has declared Him** (NKJV). And so this is Jesus—before Jerusalem, before Nazareth, before Bethlehem. Before He lived in all those places, He was the sovereign ruler of the universe.

The word translated "Lord" in our English Bibles is lowercase "ord." From the Hebrew language we understand that Isaiah is not using God's personal name, YHWH. Isaiah referred to Him as Lord, meaning, "I saw the one in charge," "I saw the ruler."

From the Life of Hezekiah:
A Picture of God's Holiness

2 Kings 18–20; 2 Chronicles 29–32; Isaiah 36–37

The multiple chapters of the Bible dedicated to the life and times of Hezekiah move like a plot line of a great war movie. There's the humble hero facing insurmountable odds against enemy armies. Just when you think there's no way out, the plot twists and good triumphs over evil. When the credits roll, you shake your head, amazed that the real hero of the story is "Almighty God—the Holy One of Israel," once again rescuing and blessing the people who are called by His name. None of the earthly empires who came up against God's people could stand against the One who sits on the throne of the universe.

Hezekiah, Israel's king **who did what was right in the eyes of the** LORD, was one of the first kings in many decades to have a vision of God on the throne of heaven (2 Kings 18:3). The bumper sticker on his royal limo could have read: "Fear nothing but God and sin," and he lived by those rules.

Hezekiah's heavenly perspective made him quick to bow to God's authority on earth. He dedicated his life to cleaning up God's house and leading God's people back to the priority of worship and holiness.

Without personal holiness, true worship is impossible. The priests in the temple repented in shame when they realized how their behavior had dishonored a holy God. This deep work of confession and repentance led to great joy in the people's newfound forgiveness. God's highway of holiness is the only road by which the downpour of God's blessing can reach us.

Hezekiah saw people who had previously not had the time or inclination to celebrate the Passover and regular times in the temple now rush to God's house. They couldn't stay away. Revival had breathed new life into what had become mechanical. Convinced that the holy God of Israel was present in their midst, their worship overflowed with a reverent awe of their Creator God.

"God is for us!" Hezekiah's confidence never shook despite the threatening, turbulent times. And the people could not hold back their worship when they traced their victory in battle back to God's promise to reward their personal persistence in fighting against sin in their own lives. Hezekiah's desire was to do all things for the praise of God's glory. That commitment not only protected them against their enemies, but it brought revival to their souls.

I saw the Lord *sitting* **upon a throne** (emphasis added). Isaiah noted that the Lord was not pacing back and forth. He was not wringing His hands. Remember, God is not like us at all. He was *sitting* upon the throne with no fear, no uncertainty, no anxiety of any kind. In the truest sense, God doesn't have a care in the world. God rules the universe with His feet up! You ask, "Why does He do that?" Because He *can*, that's why! We're not taxing Him or stretching Him in any way. When He thinks about the future, He thinks, *No problem.* He is not locked in time and space like we are. He knows the end from the beginning. He's God. He's in charge. He's holy.

> When God is recognized as being above me, beyond me, highly exalted, over me, and totally separate from me, I am getting in position for a downpour.

I saw the Lord sitting upon a throne. In a region unknown, in a realm beyond space and time where God is seen and constantly worshipped, in a place we can't go to now, but will someday very soon, God's throne is **high and lifted up.** This isn't a description of the throne's physical properties. He's not telling us how big the throne is but where it's located in heaven. Why? So even the sinless angels in heaven will understand that God is distinct and uncommon, separate, and holy. Revelation 5:11 tells us that the angels in God's throne room number ten thousand times ten thousand, and every one of them is constantly reminded of how completely separate God is because His throne is not on their level; it is "high and lifted up."

Next Isaiah observed that **the train of his robe filled the temple.** Married women reading this will have their own stories of wedding dresses that reached to the floor and more. Maybe your gown went so far behind that your bridesmaids had to help you move around. Why? Because it was a day to be honored, and the length of the dress was a symbol of splendor.

Do you know what happened on January 2, 1953? It was the coronation of Queen Elizabeth at Westminster Abbey in London, England. If you've seen the newsreels of that event, you know that the train of her robe went all the way down the aisle and out the back door of the church. *Man, who does she think she is, the queen of England?* Ah, yes she does! That's why the symbol of her splendor was over the top.

What does Scripture say about the symbol of God's splendor? The train of His robe didn't just go down the aisle; it "filled the temple"—back and forth, back and forth, doubling and redoubling until the symbol of God's holy splendor packed the house. Over and over the writers of Scripture ask, **Who is like you, O Lord?** (Exodus 15:11; Deuteronomy 33:29; Psalms 35:10; 89:8). The question is rhetorical because the answer is obvious. Who is like God? No one. That's because He is holy. He is separate. He is completely unlike us.

Heavenly Throne Room Scene #2

Let's go over now to another throne room in Ezekiel 1 where Ezekiel had a similar revelation of God on the throne. **In the thirteenth year, in the fourth month, on the fifth day of the month . . . the heavens were opened, and I saw visions of God . . . the word of the Lord came to Ezekiel . . . and the hand of the Lord was upon him there** (vv. 1–4). Ezekiel goes on for twenty-one verses to describe everything he sees in heaven except God Himself. He saves the best for last.

Ezekiel 1:26 says, **And above the expanse over their heads there was the likeness of a throne.** Anyone who's ever been to heaven talks about the throne, as we will see. **There was the likeness of a throne, in appearance like sapphire; and seated above the likeness of a throne was a likeness with a human appearance.** It's interesting that in this section of Scripture, Ezekiel uses the word *likeness* ten times and the word *appearance* sixteen times. He describes what he sees as, sort of like . . . a bit of . . . kind of like . . . He does his best, but cannot find the words for what he sees, and neither would we. The reason? You guessed it—because God is holy.

> *When I know God's place, I can know my place—then things start to fall into place.*

There is nothing to compare to the Lord. Isaiah 40:25 says, **To whom then will you compare me, that I should be like him?** Who can you compare to God? He's holy. Our words amount to a heap of inadequate comparisons . . . and I'm trying to . . . but I can't come close . . . to describing . . . God.

The text goes on in Ezekiel 1: **And upward from what had the appearance of his waist I saw as it were gleaming metal, like the appearance of fire enclosed all around. And downward from what had the appearance of his waist I saw as it were the appearance of fire, and there was brightness around him. Like the appearance of the bow that is in the cloud on the day of rain, so was the appearance of the brightness all around. Such was the appearance of the likeness of the glory of the LORD. And when I saw it, I fell on my face** (vv. 27–28).

Ezekiel was saying, "When I saw it, I had to get down low. God is high, and when I saw how exalted He is, I had to get as far from Him as possible." Why? Holiness. Holiness shouts separation. He's lofty and exalted, and we're not. Don't feel in any way that you are at all like God. Get as low as you can, as soon as possible. He is holy!

Now that is a view of God that we have lost in the church in our generation: the high, exalted, lofty, exclusive, unparalleled, unprecedented character of God. Preferring the comfort of His nearness, we have lost the reality of God's transcendent holiness. Our generation struggles and wallows in cheap grace and shallow sanctification because we have departed from the biblical picture of God's holy and exalted nature. God is not the "Man Upstairs" or "Big Daddy" or some old codger with a long white beard. God is not whatever my conscience or imagination would like Him to be. God is ineffable, indescribable glory, and He dwells in unapproachable light. **No man can see [God] and live** (Exodus 33:20 NASB). **God is a consuming fire** (Hebrews 12:29). In a single word: Holy! God is infinite holiness. When you understand that, it's not a long journey to this second aspect of God's holiness from Isaiah 6.

Holiness Demands Caution

Holiness rightly understood demands caution. Do you get it? *Be careful. Be very careful.* Isaiah has briefly described the position of the throne and the clothing of deity, but he really doesn't say anything about God Himself. Not really. He tells you about where the throne is and the train of His robe; and then he's, like, speechless, out of breath, afraid to say more. As a result, Isaiah's description moves abruptly to, "Let me tell you about the angels."

Isaiah 6:2 says, **Above him stood the seraphim.** Seraphim are angels, literally the "burning ones." Apparently they appear next to God as fire. What are they doing? They're standing, ever standing to serve the seated Sovereign.

Next Isaiah tells us, **Each had six wings.** He focuses now on a specific seraphim. **With two [wings] he covered his face,** lest they gaze upon infinite holiness and be consumed in a moment. **And with two he covered his feet.** Why? So God would not see them.

Revelation 19 tells us that the Lord's eyes are like a flame of fire. No wonder the seraph cover themselves. They don't want to look at God, and they don't want God to look at them. *Holiness, gazing at me? Not if I can help it.* But I can't. Keep in mind that the seraphs are sinless, yet they don't want heaven's holiest eyes falling upon their forms. **With two he covered his face, and with two he covered his feet, and with two he flew.** Ever serving, never seeing this sovereign God. Their motion is ceaseless as they do the bidding of Almighty God.

You can't read verse 2 without sensing in the seraphim a consuming carefulness around God. "Caution! Caution! Do what He says, exactly, immediately, totally, every time. He's God; we're not. He's holy; fly right. Don't look at Him. Cover yourself. Holiness! Caution! Holiness demands caution."

Heavenly Throne Room Scene #3

Let's go to another throne room scene and see the same thing. At the absolute end of human history, we are not surprised to find God's throne unaffected, unaltered. We enter John's vision in Revelation near the end of history. Now he refers to God's throne room again, but in a scene I hope you never attend. John describes the dead, both small and great, who are outside of Christ, standing before God at the final judgment.

Revelation 20:11 says, **Then I saw a great white throne** (there it is again). It's still there, eternal and immovable—God's throne.

The whiteness is a picture of purity. It's the same term Mark used in chapter 9 describing Jesus at the transfiguration: **Exceedingly white, as no launderer on earth can whiten** (Mark 9:3 NASB).

F. B. Meyer, the great Bible commentator who lived from 1847–1929, was visiting a woman in Scotland. She was hanging her laundry on the line and was very proud of how white the linen looked until the snow started to fall. Meyer, maybe not the most sensitive pastor in that moment,

> *God's holiness . . . puts everything and everyone in their rightful place.*

commented to the woman, "I guess your laundry doesn't look quite as white as it used to, now that the snow is falling." And she said in her lovely Scottish brogue, "Mon, what can stand against God Almighty's white?" The answer of course is that nothing can. Who can stand against the whiteness, the purity, the holiness of God? Of course God's throne is white; what other color *could* it be?

Revelation 20:11 says, **Then I saw a great white throne and him who was seated on it. From his presence** [literally, "from his face"] **earth and sky fled away, and no place was found for them.** The earth sees holiness and retreats. The sky sees holiness and pulls back.

What happens when holiness really hits home in the human heart? Second Peter 3:10 describes this time: **The day of the Lord will come like a thief, and then the heavens will pass away with a roar, and the heavenly bodies will be burned up and dissolved, and the earth and the works that are done on it will be exposed.** The point clearly is, *Caution.* When God is recognized for the infinitely holy being that He is, you don't stand around questioning His decisions. You run and hide. You get as far away and as low as you can, as fast as you can. That's God.

It always grieves me when I hear people say, "Well, if I ever meet God, I'm going to tell Him a thing or two." What are you talking about? Step away from me when you say stuff like that. Do we have any idea what we're talking about? Not if we aren't filled with fear and awful dread when we think about a genuine encounter with the God who made us all and spoke the very universe into existence.

> *When God is recognized for the infinitely holy being that He is, you don't stand around questioning His decisions.*

No one questions God. Does God do some things we don't understand? Yes. Does God do some things that we wish were different? Yes. But isn't there something inside of us that says, "I'm human, I'm fallible, I'm sinful. I don't know what's ultimately best. I don't understand how it all fits together or even what God is trying to do in a given situation." Instead I must choose to trust God. So often I say to myself, "I trust the Lord. He's awesome, He's holy. He knows what He's doing and He's doing it perfectly, on time, every time." Eternity will show the infinite, unfathomable wisdom of our almighty, holy God. You may be tempted to think, *Well He's sure doing things differently than I would do them.* Right. Remember our definition? Holy means not like us.

Speaking of the day when humanity meets holiness, Luke 23:30 says, **Then they will begin to say to the mountains, "Fall on us," and to the hills, "Cover us."** Hiding—or trying to hide—is, of course, complete futility. Rightly seen, holiness only makes you want to cover yourself. Holiness rightly understood says, "Caution, extreme caution," when talking about, thinking about, and living before a God like that.

Clean Hands and Pure Hearts—
Revival in Scotland (1949)

In 1949, two elderly women prayed daily for revival in their own lives and in the Hebrides Islands of Scotland. Faith had reached a low point in their country. They were so spiritually thirsty, they claimed God's promise, **I will pour water on the thirsty land, and streams on the dry ground** (Isaiah 44:3 HCSB). They convinced their pastor that people should ask God to quicken their hearts. He and a handful of men gathered in a barn nightly for prayer for months but with no results.

Then one day, early in the morning hours, a young man read Psalm 24:3–5: **Who may ascend the mountain of the LORD? Who may stand in His holy place? The one who has clean hands and a pure heart, who has not set his mind on what is false, and who has not sworn deceitfully. He will receive blessing from the LORD, and righteousness from the God of his salvation** (HCSB).

Speaking in his native Gaelic, the young man said: "Brethren, it seems to me just sentimental humbug to be praying as we are praying, to be waiting as we are waiting, if we ourselves are not rightly related to God." Then he asked the Lord, "Are my hands clean, is my heart pure?"* He and his fellow intercessors fell on their faces in that barn, and their lives were revived as they got their hands and hearts clean before the Lord.

Duncan Campbell, an itinerant minister, was invited to lead a series of services in their town. By Sunday of the first week, the whole island was filled with a God-consciousness. Churches were filled to overflowing. Groups and crowds met in the fields and by the roadside to get right with God. Youth left a dance at midnight to go to church. People who couldn't sleep came to church in the middle of the night to get right with God. In one Scottish community, not a home was left without someone coming to Christ.

Over the next four years, God poured waters on the thirsty ground in keeping with His promise that those with clean hands and a pure heart would receive a downpour of blessing from the Lord.

---

*Duncan Campbell, *The Price and Power of Revival: Lessons from the Hebribes Awakening* (Vinton, Va.: Christ Life Publications), 32.

Holiness Declares God's Glory

Isaiah 6:3 describes the activity of the seraphim: **And one called to another and said: "Holy, holy, holy is the Lord of hosts; the whole earth is full of his glory!"** This is the chorus that has been going on through eons of time. It's happening in heaven right now and will never cease.

> *In the truest sense, God doesn't have a care in the world. God rules the universe with His feet up!*

Think with me of all the things that God could have chosen to say about Himself in His presence. God could have called upon the seraph to sing, "Loving, loving, loving God," and it would have been true. They could chorus, "merciful, merciful, merciful," and we would say "amen." I'm guessing, though, that the seraphim probably don't have a ton of autonomy around God's throne. I'm pretty sure they do exactly what God commands them to do. Do you agree? What is spoken in the presence of God is what God most wants said and seen and understood about Himself. Those words and nothing else, ever!

God has deemed that the central, defining characteristic of His being—the word that is to be spoken in heaven, eternally and continuously, the characteristic around which all other aspects of God's nature revolve—is this: holiness. Isaiah describes two angelic lines coming out from the throne: **And one called to another.** Two lines calling out back and forth, back and forth, back and forth—an antiphonal chorus that never ceases.

In the Hebrew language, repetition shows force. If you were to say, "Well, we had quite a storm last night." It would be one thing. But if you said, "Have you been following the news? Down in the Gulf, they're having a storm-storm." That would be repetition showing force. If you wanted to amp that up a little bit and talk about the greatest hurricanes in history, you would say, "Back in the summer of 2005, Katrina hit the Gulf Coast. That was a storm-storm-storm." In the idiom of the Hebrew language, repetition shows force.

In Scripture several of God's attributes are used twice. But only regarding this attribute and only here do we see this three-peat. It's saying that God is not (just) holy. God is not (just) holy-holy. God is holy-holy-holy!

The Universe Declares God's Glory

Then, **the whole earth is full of his glory.** There is no place you can go and nothing your eyes can gaze upon that isn't this moment declaring the fact of God's existence and His exaltation over what He has made. All created things shout the existence of the Creator. Everything that is designed shouts the existence of the Master Designer. All that we see and experience has and continues to flow from the infinite holiness and creative genius of Almighty God. It means that **no creature is hidden from his sight** (Hebrews 4:13.) God's glory is revealed because He made it. Let's think about that for a moment.

The weather system is full of His glory. Think of the awesome energy of Hurricane Katrina. Scientists tell us that Katrina's energy was comparable to twenty times the energy of the bomb that was dropped on Hiroshima. Extreme weather is measured in the thousands of people it kills, the millions who go without power, and the hundreds of billions of dollars it will take to repair the ravaged area of our country. No wonder they're called "acts of God." Storms are, of course, a muted display of God's glory. The engine that drives those kinds of storms is only a fractional representation of God's reality. It's a manifestation of holy power that performs these things on this tiny sphere we call earth.

The earth is full of His glory. Some would think that God isn't taking care of the world, but how wrong it is to think that. Did you know that the earth's axis is perfectly situated for life on this earth? Our planet sits on an angle of twenty-three degrees in relation to the sun. If that were adjusted just slightly, even two degrees, the entire earth would be covered with a polar ice cap. There would be no life at all on earth unless God's hand were holding it at this perfect angle.

Preferring the comfort of His nearness, we have lost the reality of God's transcendent holiness.

Our solar system is full of His glory. Our sun is so massive that it could fit 1.3 million of our earths inside it. It may not look that big, but it is. It hangs in space ninety-three million miles away from us—and that's just in our solar system. The Bible says that God sustains the universe. By His power, all things are created and sustained. Colossians 1:17 says, **In him all things hold together.** The earth is full of His glory.

Pluto is so far away that it was undiscovered until seventy-five years ago. Our galaxy, the Milky Way, is so expansive it would take one thousand lifetimes traveling at the speed of light just to cross it. And relatively speaking, all of this stuff is in our backyard. Our galaxy contains planets that we could call "just the boys in the neighborhood."

The universe is full of His glory. Astronomers number galaxies at 140 billion in the universe. (Yeah, as if they counted them.) Can we imagine how many a billion is? No, it's really beyond our comprehension. It would take 140 billion peas to fill Chicago's Soldier Field stadium, with every single pea representing a galaxy. Our solar system is only a tiny part of just one galaxy. God stood in eternity past and **spoke, and the worlds were formed** (Hebrews 11:3). Who is like you, O Lord?

Forget the Telescope; Look in the Mirror

Augustine, one of the church fathers, rightly observed that "men go abroad to wonder at the height of mountains, at the huge waves of the sea, at the long courses of the river, at the vast compass of the ocean, at the circle motion of the stars; and they pass by themselves without wondering at all." The human body declares the glory of God with greater volume than a galaxy ever could.

What God has created in the human body staggers the mind. Each of us has one hundred thousand miles of blood vessels— enough to reach around the earth three times. Our hearts beat one hundred thousand times every day. (You probably aren't even working on that; yet it still is happening right now, thank God.) Your body creates twenty-five million new cells every second. Nerve impulses travel 426 feet per second—five times faster than lightning—coursing through your body. A three-month-old unborn baby already has detailed fingerprints. It's true what Psalm 139:14 says: We are **fearfully and wonderfully made.** Our intricately designed bodies are shouting the workmanship of a Master Designer.

HOLY—Not Like Us!

Can you keep the earth perfectly tilted? Can you keep the planets and the stars moving in a galactic choreography that staggers the mind? Can you do that? If God were to say, "I'm not doing it anymore," do you have someone to suggest who might take over for Him? There is no one like Him. He is holy. He is unparalleled. He is unprecedented. He is first, and no one else even rates a distant second. Words fail in helping us to comprehend the unalterable, incomprehensible holiness of God. How right the seraphim are to be singing this moment, **Holy, holy, holy is the** Lord **of hosts; the whole earth is full of his glory.** Everywhere we turn we see the fingerprints of God. The revelation of the reality of the God of the universe—the One who made it all—declares His glory.

Heavenly Throne Room Scene #4

Let me take you to another throne room scene, just to push this idea a little further. John's heavenly vision is only beginning in Revelation 4:1–9.

> **After this I looked, and behold, a door standing open in heaven! And the first voice, which I had heard speaking to me like a trumpet, said, "Come up here, and I will show you what must take place after this." At once I was in the Spirit, and behold, a throne stood in heaven, with one seated on the throne. And he who sat there had the appearance of jasper** [that's like quartz] **and carnelian** [kind of a reddish-brown stone]**, and around the throne was a rainbow that had the appearance of an emerald.** [The point is not the appearance of the jewels, but that these are the most precious jewels of John's day and he's comparing these to the Lord. Notice the similarities of these descriptions: the throne, God

seated, the rainbow.] **Around the throne were twenty-four thrones, and seated on the thrones were twenty-four elders, clothed in white garments, with golden crowns on their heads.**

From the throne came flashes of lightning, and rumblings and peals of thunder, and before the throne were burning seven torches of fire, which are the seven spirits of God. [Some suggest that the number seven in Scripture is a picture of fullness or completeness as in Daniel's reference to seventy days in Daniel 9:24. Others believe the seven spirits refers to Isaiah 11:2: And the Spirit of the LORD shall rest upon him, the Spirit of wisdom and understanding, the Spirit of counsel and might, the Spirit of knowledge and the fear of the LORD.]

And before the throne there was as it were a sea of glass, like crystal. And around the throne, on each side of the throne, are four living creatures, full of eyes in front and behind: the first living creature like a lion, the second living creature like an ox, the third living creature with the face of a man, and the fourth living creature like an eagle in flight. And the four living creatures, each of them with six wings, are full of eyes all around and within, and day and night they never cease to say, "Holy, holy, holy, is the Lord God Almighty, who was and is and is to come!" [Does this remind you of Isaiah 6?]

And whenever the living creatures give glory and honor and thanks to him who is seated on the throne, who lives forever and ever, the twenty-four elders fall

down before him who is seated on the throne and worship him who lives forever and ever. They cast their crowns before the throne.

Why off with the crowns? Because no one, rightly viewing God's holy throne room, wants to be associated with honor. No honor to me; all honor to Him. He's holy. He doesn't share His glory. **Not to us, O LORD . . . but to your name give glory** (Psalm 115:1).

John adds to our understanding of the angelic chorus: **Worthy are you, our Lord and God** (Revelation 4:11). The word translated "worthy" was used of properly balanced scales. If the weight of the precious metal was equivalent to the standard weight, it was considered worthy—it balanced out. When Scripture says God is worthy, it means that there is no amount of praise that we can place upon Him that somehow tips the scales. He is worthy and measures perfectly with everything that we can say and give to Him. We can't come close to overdoing our expression of praise and worship.

Sincere worship, given from the heart, is never over the top, or too much, because He is worthy. It will always balance out. Isn't that a cool word? *Worthy* **are you, our Lord and God, to receive glory and honor and power, for you created all things, and by your will they existed and were created** (Revelation 4:11, emphasis added).

Holiness describes separation. It demands caution. It declares glory. And finally, holiness determines mystery.

Holiness Determines Mystery

Let's return to Isaiah 6: **And the foundations of the thresholds shook at the voice of him who called, and the house was**

filled with smoke (v. 4). Isaiah, at the door to the throne room, no doubt prostrate by now, feels the entire room begin to shake as the Lord speaks. What the Lord said we do not know, but it must have been a call for the vision to end because Isaiah's vision was immediately shrouded by smoke.

The Bible says that God sustains the universe. By His power, all things are created and sustained.

If you're like me, you have to wonder why all the shaking? Why the smoke? Why the audible call that the audience must end? Here's why: holiness always says, "This far; no further. This close; no closer. This part you get to know; this part though you can't even comprehend." There's always a mystery at the center of holiness. Inevitably, God sets up a perimeter and halts our progress on the outskirts of holiness.

In Revelation 10:4–7, John was writing like mad everything that the Spirit showed him. Suddenly the Lord gave the command, **Do not write it down.** John may have thought, *Well, I just saw it, and I want to write it down.* "No, don't!" God has placed limits on what He wants us to know about Him. Revelation 10 goes on to describe the day when the trumpet will sound and all mystery will be revealed. Someday Christ will return, and those who love the Lord will go to be with Him. Only then will the mystery be removed. Then we will know fully even as we are known, says 1 Corinthians 13:12. It will be a time promised in 1 John 3:2: **We shall be like him, because we shall see him as he is.**

For now, however, as long as we're living on earth, as long as we're in these imperfect bodies, there will be a certain amount of mystery. This far and no further—that's why Isaiah saw the foundations shaking, heard the voice calling out, and saw the house filling with smoke. That's it—no more. Mystery. In our humanness we can't handle all His holiness; so God, in mercy, raises the veil and dwells in mystery.

Now we'll visit that final throne room that confirms the reality—no, the necessity—of mystery. Daniel is the other human messenger who was given a view of this holy throne room. Daniel 7:9 begins, **As I looked, thrones were placed, and the Ancient of days** [isn't that an awesome name for God?] **took his seat; his clothing was white as snow.** Have you noticed how these passages are somewhat similar? Isn't it interesting that the writers of Scripture, living hundreds of years apart—men who never knew one another and most of whom didn't even read each other's writings—all report the very same things? Why is that? Because what they were seeing is real, and they were really seeing it. **And the hair of his head like pure wool; his throne was fiery flames; its wheels were burning fire.** [Mystery!] **A stream of fire issued and came out from before him.** [Mystery!] **A thousand thousands served him, and ten thousand times ten thousand stood before him.** [Mystery!] **The court sat in judgment, and the books were opened.** You may wonder, "What books?" You don't know about the books? You definitely need to know about the books.

Revelation 20 explains: **Then I saw a great white throne and him who was seated on it. From his presence earth and sky fled away, and no place was found for them. And I saw the dead, great and small, standing before the throne, and books were opened. Then another book was opened, which is the book of**

> *Sincere worship, given from the heart, is never over the top, or too much, because He is worthy.*

life . . . And if anyone's name was not found written in the book of life, he was thrown into the lake of fire (vv. 11–12, 15).

Is your name in the book of life? Careful—it's really easy to give the right answer. Keep in mind that your name is not in the book of life just because you say it's there. You can't tell God to put it there. Your name is in the book of life because you meet the soul conditions for the new birth. Have you recognized your sinful, fallen condition before a holy God? Have you turned from your sin, rejecting that old lifestyle, and given your life to Jesus Christ and to Him alone? Can you say from your heart that He is your reason for living now? Has He become to you everything you love and long for, your very reason for life itself? That's what it means to be transformed by the power of the gospel.

You can't fool God. If He's not "the pearl of great price" to you (Matthew 13:46 NKJV), if He's not the treasure of your affection in increasing measure, then your name is not in the book. Matthew 7:22–23 says that many people will say on that day, **"Lord, Lord, did we not prophesy in your name, and cast out demons in your name, and do many mighty works in your name?"** And Jesus will say, **"I never knew you; depart from me."**

You don't know the Lord because you say you do or because your mom says you do or because your pastor says you do. You can be sure you know the Lord when your life, your behavior, your actions and attitudes confirm that you do. **If anyone is in Christ, he is a new creation. The old has passed away; behold, the new has come** (2 Corinthians 5:17).

There are no perfect people reading or writing this, but we must be people who are changing day by day. Our testimonies should be, "I don't talk to my wife the way I used to. I don't go where I used to go. I stopped looking at things that made me feel guilty and ashamed. I used to be addicted to a certain substance that calmed my nerves and took the edge off; now I'm in Christ and there is no edge. I am free from what used to enslave me. I'm free in Christ. The power of sin is broken in me and I'm changing, day by day by day. My language is different, my thoughts are higher, my priorities are better, my purpose is beyond myself. I've been born again."

That's the story of a person whose name is in the book of life. Is that your story? Is your name in that book? If not, you're not ready to stand before a holy God. You must turn. By faith, turn from sin and to God. (Turn back to page 6 to know how to ask God for this new relationship.) If you do know and love the Lord, never let God's holiness get far from your focus. Remember who He really is and what it means to account to this God of infinite, indescribable holiness.

The Great Awakening

The Great Awakening in America happened during the 1730s and 1740s. It swept up and down the Atlantic seaboard from Nova Scotia to Atlanta, Georgia. Conversions in the colonies increased more than fourfold.

One of the key men whom God used during the Great Awakening was Jonathan Edwards. He was tall and thin and unimpressive in his oratory skills, reading his hour-long sermons to his congregation from his notes. Yet he possessed a deep and profound belief in the holiness of God and the reality of hell for any person who would pass into eternity without Jesus Christ.

His most famous sermon was "Sinners in the Hands of an Angry God." He first preached it on July 8, 1741, in Enfield, Massachusetts, and it marked the beginning of the Great Awakening in New England. The point of his message was to awaken people to the utmost holiness of God and the need to be reconciled with Him. During the sermon, sinners in the audience evoked groanings, pleas for him to stop preaching, and even fainting among them as they listened. An eyewitness, Steven Williams, reported, "We went over to Enfield to hear Mr. Edwards who preached a most awakening message. Before the sermon was done there was a great moaning and crying throughout the whole house. 'What shall I do to be saved? Oh, I'm going to hell! What shall I do for Christ?' The minister was obliged to desist, the shrieks and the cries were so piercing."

Here is a brief quote from that sermon. Be patient with the old style of writing and read it for its message:

> The wrath of God is like great waters that are dammed for the present; they increase more and more, and rise higher and higher, till an outlet is given; and the longer the stream is stopped, the more rapid and mighty is its course, when once it is let loose. It is true, that judgment against your evil works has not been executed hitherto; the floods of God's vengeance have been withheld; but your guilt in the mean time is constantly increasing, and you are every day treasuring up more wrath; the waters are constantly rising, and waxing more and more mighty; and there is nothing but the mere pleasure of God, that holds the waters back, that are unwilling to be stopped, and press hard to go forward. If God should only withdraw his hand from the flood-gate, it would immediately fly open, and the fiery floods of the fierceness and wrath of God would rush forth with inconceivable fury, and would come upon you with omnipotent power; and if

your strength were ten thousand times greater than it is, yea, ten thousand times greater than the strength of the stoutest, sturdiest devil in hell, it would be nothing to withstand or endure it.

The bow of God's wrath is bent, and the arrow made ready on the string, and justice bends the arrow at your heart, and strains the bow, and it is nothing but the mere pleasure of God, and that of an angry God, without any promise or obligation at all, that keeps the arrow one moment from being made drunk with your blood.

In our humanness we can't handle all His holiness; so God, in mercy, raises the veil and dwells in mystery.

Thus all you that never passed under a great change of heart, by the mighty power of the Spirit of God upon your souls; all you that were never born again, and made new creatures, and raised from being dead in sin, to a state of new, and before altogether unexperienced light and life, are in the hands of an angry God. However you may have reformed your life in many things, and may have had religious affections, and may keep up a form of religion in your families and closets, and in the house of God, it is nothing but his mere pleasure that keeps you from being this moment swallowed up in everlasting destruction. However unconvinced you may now be of the truth of what you hear, by and by you will be fully convinced of it. Those that are gone from being in the like circumstances with you, see that it was so with them; for destruction came suddenly upon most of them; when they expected nothing of it, and while they were saying, Peace and safety: now they see, that those things on which they depended for peace and safety were nothing but thin air and empty shadows.

This is what God's holiness means to us right now. You cannot fool Him, trick Him, or play games with Him like we are tempted to do at times. God is holy; He is not like us. You may have a way of getting out of jams, using your skill with words or your winsome way. Such approaches are worthless before the holy God who made you. He knows perfectly the true condition of your soul.

This is where revival begins. God on the throne: a picture of holiness.

Turn from your sin, and your self, and your pleasure-seeking, and your "look at me; aren't I a good boy?" and all of your reputation and self-consuming godlessness. Turn from these empty things and embrace Christ by faith as the great treasure of your soul. Turn.

For those who have made that turning and have experienced life in Christ, hear with me the call to return, **Come, let us return to the LORD,** as the great prize and object of our life and affections. Let us return to the Lord, the God of infinite holiness.

Gather up in your mind, in your heart, and in your strength what the Lord has been saying to you as you have read this chapter. Keep in mind that the Word of God is a seed that has been planted in your spirit today. The Bible says the enemy would come to snatch away the seed that has been sown in your heart. You could have it out of your mind before you close this book. But God's desire is that this seed will be nurtured with further meditation, prayer, reflection, and study so that it might grow up into life and faith and obedience to Him.

This is where revival begins. God on the throne: a picture of holiness.

ACTIVATE

Alone with God

1. Get completely alone. Shut off anything that could distract you. Close all doors. Get on your face before God—lie flat on the floor. This isn't the time to make any requests of God. Now is the time to humble yourself before Him, acknowledging His holiness.

2. Tell Him in your own words: "I now see You, Lord, high and lifted up, beyond any previous image I had of You. I worship You in the beauty of Your holiness. How great You are; how completely beyond anything of this world. Why do You even think of me? Help me grasp what it's like to stand before Your holiness."

3. Stay in this prayer position longer than is comfortable. Ask God to help you keep your focus on Him. Return to this place again. When you face up to God's glory, you find yourself face down in worship.

ELEVATE

Lord, thank You for a fresh view of Your exalted holy nature. Great God of the universe, holy and high, lifted up. I exalt You, Lord. You are the object of my greatest thoughts, the end of my deepest affections. I give myself wholly to You and to You alone. Revive me according to Your Word even as I bow. I ask in Jesus' strong name. Amen.

REPLICATE

Helping Each Other Share Christ

Get with a friend who loves the Lord and discuss the following:

1. How is this message about God's holiness one of the most loving things you could tell someone?

2. Imagine this message of God's holiness is all you knew about God. How would you feel? What would it be like then to hear about Jesus and His offer of salvation?

3. Why do you think this doctrine has been more widely known and accepted in past generations and yet it is such a new concept to our generation?

Brainstorm together on how to tell someone you know about the holiness of God, as well as His invitation to come to Him for salvation by grace through faith. Discuss simple statements you can make that would open the conversation about how to get right with God.

For the wrath of God is revealed from heaven

against all ungodliness and unrighteousness of men,

who by their unrighteousness suppress the truth.

For what can be known about God is plain to them,

because God has shown it to them. For his invisible

attributes, namely, his eternal power and divine nature,

have been clearly perceived, ever since the creation of

the world, in the things that have been made. So they

are without excuse. For although they knew God,

they did not honor him as God or give thanks to him,

but they became futile in their thinking,

and their foolish hearts were darkened.

ROMANS 1:18–21

CHAPTER 3

Sin in the Mirror:
A Picture of Brokenness

Does anybody like going to the doctor? No, but we do it because we know that if we have a problem, we need it diagnosed, treated, and out of our lives. What good would it do if the doctor saw a big, dark spot on our x-ray and sent us home, telling us that everything was fine? "Oh, I wanted to tell them the truth, but I knew it would ruin their day to know they have cancer," the doctor might rationalize.

In some ways, a correct diagnosis is a relief no matter how serious the prognosis. Now we know what we need to go after. *Do the surgery, Doc. Get it all!*

In the last chapter we visited the throne room of heaven and got a fresh view of the holy, exalted God of the universe. Have you ever seen that view of God before? Maybe it was the first time you realized how far above and beyond us in every conceivable way God actually is. Wholly apart from us. Holy!

Understanding holiness and how incredibly high God has set the standard for human behavior makes His command for us to **be holy, for I am holy** (1 Peter 1:16) totally overwhelming. It reveals to us how pitifully ravaged we are by sin and what our lives have become. There's no way any of us could compare ourselves to God's holy stature. We're desperately riddled with the cancer of sin. Unless we embrace an aggressive treatment plan, it's terminal.

"Wait a minute," you say. "I'm a Christian! Jesus forgave my sins." Yes, He did. Christ paid the full price for your redemption. Through faith in Him your salvation is secure. That's the eternal picture, but don't make the mistake so many Christians do by confusing salvation with sanctification. The former deals with your eternal standing before God in Christ; the latter deals with God's post-conversion work in you today. What are you allowing God to do about sin in your life *today?* Even though you have been forgiven and saved by the work of Jesus Christ, there remains in you a definite bent toward doing things your own way. God wants sin out of your life because it's the only thing that keeps you from experiencing the torrential downpour of blessing He wants to rain upon you.

> *God wants sin out of your life because it's the only thing that keeps you from experiencing the torrential downpour of blessing He wants to rain upon you.*

We have learned in Hosea 6 about God's readiness to open the windows of heaven and pour down His blessing on the parched ground of our hearts. We know that will happen only as we return to Him, which begins by seeing the sin in your life for what it is—a barrier.

Drop the Umbrella

Sin is like an umbrella. God's grace can be pouring down all around you, even blessing your family or friends at church, but all that God is giving fails to fall upon you because of sin. Like a big umbrella held high over your head, sin blocks the showers of blessing from reaching your life.

You can study the Bible until your head explodes or serve in the Sunday school until the church wants to hire you full time, but in the end your relationship with God is just about one thing: putting away your sin. If you are not dealing with it as God prescribes, your spiritual arteries are going to be clogged and no amount of study or service will get the blood pumping consistently. That's the bottom line. You have to deal with sin God's way.

Are You Talking to Me?

Trust me when I tell you that the content of this book was impacting me long before I had the privilege of writing it down for you. However I'm not going to weaken the impact of this section by talking about me or your neighbor. I am asking God to take these words straight to *your* heart. It's understood that we all need this message. O.K.?

It's *your* sin that hinders you from experiencing a downpour of revival. Not sin in the neighborhood, not sin in the newspaper, but sin in the mirror. Sin is the answer to your (perhaps private) questions, "Why don't I feel close to God the way I used to? What happened to my passion for God?" Sin is what's in the way.

For the most part, evangelical Christians are good at seeing sin on television and in the church lobby, but we fail miserably at seeing sin in the mirror. **The heart is deceitful above all things, and desperately sick; who can understand it?** (Jeremiah 17:9). Our capacity to deceive ourselves leads us to believe we are holier than we really are. Our sinful hearts trick us into thinking that "everyone else has problems, but not me." As one preacher rightly asserts, "You're being lied to and it's an inside job." It's your own heart that lies to you about personal sin—and that deception is death to downpour.

Take Sin Seriously

I doubt you've ever heard anyone say, "Well, what's a little cancer? Let it go."

If we don't see the horror of sin and God's holy intensity about sin, we'll never be able to rightly comprehend or understand why it needs to be taken so seriously. Sin brings God's wrath.

Romans 1:18 says, **For the wrath of God is revealed from heaven against all ungodliness and unrighteousness of men, who by their unrighteousness suppress the truth.**

After the glory of Jesus Christ, who is the solution to sin, the next most dominant theme in Scripture is sin itself. More than two thousand times, various "syn"onyms are used in the Bible that refer to sin, ungodliness, wickedness, or unrighteousness. On every page, in every chapter, this unconquerable human condition is described in horrific detail.

Romans 1:18–29 is the central passage in Scripture that outlines the serious effects of sin. If you're committed to the goal of personal revival in your life, then you need to get your Bible and open it to this passage and follow as we learn what God has to say about your sin.

Sin Defined

Sin is any failure to conform to God's standard from His Word—in action, in failure to act, or in attitude. The Hebrew word is *hata;* the Greek word is *hamartia.* Both these words mean "to miss the mark," as in an archer's target, but of course God doesn't play games. Sin is much more serious than "Oops, I didn't get a bull's-eye." Or "Uh-oh, missed again; I really stink at this." No, sin is not a game. It's the reason for every dark human experience. It's the reason Christ's death was necessary. Romans 6:23 says, **The wages of sin is death.**

You have to deal with sin God's way.

The Origin of Our Sin

Many of the problems, struggles, and fears that you face today are because of what happened in the Garden of Eden in those very first days of history. Adam and Eve chose to go their own way. In Genesis 2:16–17 God told them, **"You may surely eat of every tree of the garden, but of the tree of the knowledge of good and evil you shall not eat, for in the day that you eat of it you shall surely die."** They were created with the freedom to choose, and they chose the only thing God forbade. According to Genesis 3:6–7, **When the woman saw that the tree was good for food, and that it was a delight to the eyes, and that the tree was to be desired to make one wise, she took of its fruit and ate; and she also gave some to her husband who was with her, and he ate. Then the eyes of both were opened, and they knew that they were naked.** They surrendered their innocence to sin.

The Bible teaches that Adam and Eve passed their sin nature, like a bad gene, to all of mankind. Romans 5:12, 19 report, **Therefore, just as sin came into the world through one man, and death through sin, and so death spread to all men . . . by the one man's disobedience the many were made sinners.** David said in Psalm 51:5, **Behold, I was brought forth in iniquity, and in sin did my mother conceive me.** Apart from God's grace, the intent of our heart is **only evil continually** (Genesis 6:5).

As harsh as it sounds, that makes every unbeliever an enemy of God. We do not have to do anything to become God's enemies; we are born that way (see Romans 5:10; Colossians 1:21; James 4:4). The New Testament refers to those without Christ as **children of wrath** (Ephesians 2:3; see also John 3:36). Every person born into this world is born with an inclination to sin. That's the first theological category: the origin of sin.

The Extent of Our Sin

Just how far does this sin nature reach? (Hint: to the core.)

1. *Everybody is a sinner.* Ecclesiastes 7:20 says, **Surely there is not a righteous man on earth who does good and never sins.** Romans 3:23 echoes, **For all have sinned and fall short of the glory of God.**

2. *To claim otherwise is self-deceit.* First John 1:8, 10 teaches, **If we say we have no sin, we deceive ourselves, and the truth is not in us . . . If we say we have not sinned, we make him a liar, and his word is not in us.**

3. Even the apostles acknowledged sin. The apostle Paul writes in Romans 7:18, **For I know that nothing good dwells in me, that is, in my flesh. For I have the desire to do what is right, but not the ability to carry it out.**

4. *Even those not obviously sinful are still sinners.* First Timothy 5:24 proves, **The sins of some men are conspicuous, going before them to judgment, but the sins of others appear later.**

O.K. So we've all got a sin problem. Yes, and it's a slippery slope. Let's continue our study of the most common subject of Scripture with a look at where sin takes us.

The Intent of Sin

1. *Sin will pursue you.* Before Cain murdered his brother Abel, God told him, **"If you do not do well, sin is crouching at the door. Its desire is for you, but you must rule over it."** Cain did not heed the warning, and sin pursued and conquered him (Genesis 4:7, 11–12).

2. *Sin will disappoint you.* Hebrews 11:25 says that **the pleasures of sin are only for a season.** Time will run out—and misery will be waiting on the other side. Sin will always disappoint you; don't allow yourself to believe otherwise.

> Sin will always disappoint you; never allow yourself to believe otherwise.

3. *Sin will trip you up.* Hebrews 12:1 says, **Let us lay aside every weight, and the sin which so easily ensnares us** (NKJV). You're going along doing pretty well, and suddenly you're flat on your face. Satan will spot your weakness and set sin under your feet. If you don't lay aside the opportunity to sin, you will eventually, inevitably crash. Sin trips you up.

4. *Sin will enslave you.* Paul tells us in Romans 6:16 that sin is addictive: **Do you not know that if you present yourselves to anyone as obedient slaves, you are slaves of the one whom you obey, either of sin, which leads to death, or of obedience, which leads to righteousness?** You are the slave of the one you obey. When sin whispers in your ear, "Do it, do it, do it" and you lean in to listen, you are on the pathway to addiction.

5. *Sin will expose you.* Don't be fooled. Proverbs 28:13 says, **Whoever conceals his transgressions will not prosper.** Numbers 32:23 affirms, **Be sure your sin will find you out.** If you're sitting on a secret as you read this book . . . newsflash!—it's coming out!

You had better deal with it soon. Yes, it's embarrassing, but all the worse if someone must force you to see it.

Sin will pursue you, disappoint you, trip you up, enslave you, and ultimately it will expose you. No wonder sin brings God's wrath.

Why Is the World So Messed Up?

Romans 1:18 says, **For the wrath of God is revealed from heaven against all ungodliness and unrighteousness.** That term *ungodliness* means to disrespect faith, to think lowly of all things that are spiritual. *Unrighteousness* is the idea of pushing aside what is right. Notice again verse 18. The wrath of God— God's deep-seated, burning, holy anger against sin—is revealed from heaven.

There's something inside each of us that demands and calls out for justice. If we see a wrong being done, like someone stealing a woman's purse, or butting in line at the bank, or trying to hurt an innocent person, most of us feel a surge of anger rising within us. This is true because we are made in God's image. Even though our hearts are sinful and selfish, we feel a righteous anger toward the wrong done. How much more then is the anger of an infinitely holy God when we choose to break His law? Notice that the word *revealed* in the original tense carries the idea of ongoing action. The wrath of God is *being* revealed in our world today; it's happening right now.

You cannot explain the injustice and heartache that is broadcast on every form of media from every corner of the world without a proper theology of sin. You cannot explain what God allows, promotes, and causes in this world if you don't comprehend the holiness of God and the wrath of God directed against

From the Life of David:
A Picture of Brokenness
Psalm 51; 2 Samuel 12

How did I end up over here? King David probably wondered that as he put down the mirror that Nathan had held in front of him. His entire life had been marked by a faith and trust that burned hot after God. Who was this prodigal in the mirror?

How many times had David cried out for God in the crucible and God had refined him like gold? How many private conversations had he had with the lover of his soul on the slopes of Bethlehem, tending sheep? In the caves of En Gedi on the run from Saul? Coming home from battle with the songs of triumph ringing in his ears?

How long has it been since I've known that spiritual victory? Since I've felt that close to God? What happened to the joy of my salvation?

That's what Nathan had come to help David answer. Somewhere along the way, David's slight compromises, the lost priorities, the increasing distance from God, had slowly dried up his heart. Sin had done what sin will always do. And the best worship leader in the history of Israel had been quieted.

David knew now what needed to be done, and it was something only God could accomplish. David needed new life breathed into his spirit. He needed a downpour of forgiveness to wash over his dry and thirsty soul. For the first time in a long time, David understood that the path to revival began with his turning around. Psalm 51 records his willingness:

Have mercy on me, O God. *Deal with this sin in my life, Lord. I come on Your terms.*

My sin is ever before me. *What I have ignored, dismissed, and rationalized is now staring me in the face. It's my sin. It's my fault.*

Against you, you only, have I sinned. *You are a righteous and holy God. This sin has hurt Your name. I've caused others to misunderstand Your holiness.*

Create in me a clean heart, O God. *Do the surgery, Lord. Get it all.*

The sacrifices of God are . . . a broken and contrite heart. *The one thing You require is the only thing I can offer, Lord. Here I am—shattered by my sin and what it has cost You. Please make me whole again.*

Renew a right spirit within me. *Help me to stay in this place until Your work is complete. Please make my heart alive again.*

Restore to me the joy of your salvation. *Revive me, Lord.*

And God did bring revival to David's soul—as God promises to do for every broken heart that comes to Him in humility and faith.

sin. And if you understand what Scripture says about the end times, then you know that as far as God's wrath is concerned we "ain't seen nothing yet." It's how holiness feels about sin. Sin brings God's wrath.

No Excuses

I don't know about you, but all this talk about sin is making me feel kinda sick. Can't we move on to the solution? Not yet. Not until this theology of sin invades our own lives. "But my sin isn't hurting anyone. How could it be so wrong when it feels so right? It's not like I'm the only one to ever struggle with this."

The universality of our rationalizations reveals the commonness of our struggle. Each of us has little phrases we repeat to ourselves when we feel the slightest touch of conviction. Wake up! Don't be deceived. Downpour is only a pipe dream until you admit that God's primary interest is not your skill in diagnosing the sin of others. He wants to get *you* into surgery. Having freed you from the penalty of sin for all of eternity through your faith in Jesus, God wants to go after the power of sin in your life, here and now. Romans 6:14 says, **For sin will have no dominion over you, since you are not under law but under grace.**

Why Won't God Just Eliminate Sin?

Some people argue that if God didn't want sin in the world, He should have made a world where there was no sin. Oh sure, He could have made us robots. Instead, God made a world in which we have the freedom to choose, knowing that many would reject Him and a few would choose to give their affections in worship to the One who made it all. God would rather have the meaningful worship of a few rather than the robotic worship of the masses. Nobody wants coerced affection, least of all God. Genuine worship and love from the souls of a few—that's the choice that God made.

And because God created a world in which we are free to choose, I am responsible for my own sinful choices. Romans 1:18 makes it clear that no one chooses my sin but me: **Who by their unrighteousness suppress the truth.** That word *suppress* means to hold down. Sin stiff-arms and squelches God. Sin suppresses the flow of God's favor toward me. Every choice to do wrong, every choice to leave the good undone, every wrong attitude perpetuated and promoted in my life is a choice to push God away—and it's called sin.

> *Every choice to do wrong, every choice to leave the good undone, every wrong attitude perpetuated and promoted in my life is a choice to push God away— and it's called sin.*

Sin Suppresses the Fact of God's Existence

You may have heard about the boy who stood holding a string that went up into the clouds. A passerby asked him, "What are you doing?"

"I'm flying a kite," the boy said.

"Well, how do you know? You can't see the kite."

"Well, every so often I feel the tug on the string."

It's like that with God, isn't it? I've never seen God, but I sure feel the tug on the string. That's the God-consciousness in each of us.

According to Barna research, 69 percent of people admit they believe there is a God.* Why? Because it's in our hearts. Think of

*www.barna.org/FlexPage.aspx?Page=Topic&TopicID=2

the most evil, dastardly person you've ever heard of. Deep within that person's heart is a suppressed awareness of the existence of God. It's there in all of us. Maybe science will one day discover the "God gene," but either way this inherent knowledge of God's existence is there because God put it there. Ecclesiastes 3:11 states that God has **put eternity into man's heart.**

Theologians call this "God-consciousness." You've got to work hard to suppress that sense of "somebody's there. He sees me right now. He's keeping track." Do you have a sense of that? God put that in you. When you get away from God and embrace a life of sin, you hold that God-consciousness down. The truth is **suppressed in unrighteousness.** When I choose a life of sin, I suppress that inherent knowledge; I push it down.

Sin Is My Choice: My Conscience Accuses Me

Beyond your heart knowledge of God, God has given to each of us a conscience—an internal alarm about what's right and wrong. Everyone is born with a conscience. None of us can plead ignorance. We can't show up in heaven someday and say, "Oh, I'm so sorry, God. I didn't know." Romans 1:19 says, **For what can be known about God is plain to them, because God has shown it to them.** I love that. What can be known about God is clearly seen. It's evident to us because God has woven it into our conscience. God made you to know some things about Him. He wrote it on our hearts.

Look at Romans 2:14–15: **For when Gentiles, who do not have the law, by nature do what the law requires, they are a law to themselves, even though they do not have the law. They show that the work of the law is *written on their hearts*, while their conscience also bears witness, and their conflict-**

ing thoughts accuse or even excuse them (emphasis added). That's conscience.

Can you let your conscience be your guide? No, you cannot. First, your conscience is conditioned by what you know. The more you're in God's Word, the more tender your conscience gets. Second, your conscience is conditioned by what you do. The more you do right, the more tenderhearted you become. The more you do wrong, the more calloused and hard you become. That's why 1 Timothy 4:2 says that your conscience can actually become seared or lose its capacity to feel pain. If you feel no twinge of guilt about sin, it's because your conscience has been seared. Eventually some people become pathological and criminally evil because they silenced their conscience through repeated sin.

Sin Is My Choice: My Creator Convicts Me

Not only does my conscience convict me; God Himself convicts me that I'm going to answer for the choices I make. Romans 1:20 says, **For his invisible attributes, namely, his eternal power and divine nature, have been clearly perceived, ever since the creation of the world, in the things that have been made. So they are without excuse.**

I was playing golf with a couple of guys this week who are a lot better golfers than I am. I wasn't hitting the ball very well—sometimes it went left, sometimes right. (I think I need new clubs.) But honestly, it's not the tools; it's the tradesman. The problem isn't the golf club; the problem is the golfer. There can be no bad shots without a bad golfer. It's the law of cause and effect. It's a basic law of the universe.

The idea of there being an effect without a cause is the height of foolishness. That's what Romans 1:20 says: **For his invisible**

The Derksen Brothers
and the Canadian Revival (1971)

Sam and Arnold Derksen had been feuding for thirteen years. Although the brothers attended the same church, they had not spoken for two years. When Sam walked down one aisle of the church, his brother walked out the other, or vice versa. All their bitterness had erupted because of their mutual involvement in the music program of the church. They had different ideas, different tastes, and above all, a different evaluation of each other's ability. They were so adept at concealing their mutual hatred that many people did not even know the hostility existed.

Sam believed reconciliation was hopeless. They had tried to patch up their differences before and failed. There was no reason to think that their bitterness could be resolved now. But God was at work.

One night, following the evening service, Arnold went to the basement of the church with the pastor and a deacon. The three men suggested that Sam join them. He agreed to do so, since he was deeply convicted about his attitude. But when he asked Arnold to forgive him, the reply was icy, "Well, it's about time!" Sam was disillusioned. The episode confirmed his suspicions that they could not be reunited.

Rather than let the brothers go, the pastor and deacon prayed. A few moments later, God shattered Arnold's haughty spirit. He broke under the conviction of the Holy Spirit and confessed his sins, crying to God for mercy. A member sitting in the auditorium said that he could hear the men praying, crying, and beating on the downstairs wall. A few moments later, the brothers asked each other's forgiveness, wept, and embraced. They emerged walking hand-in-hand as they approached their waiting families. There was hugging, kissing, and laughing.

The next night, the brothers sang a duet. Later, they traveled to a nearby city in the same car to share what God had done in their lives. They rejoiced and thanked God that He had delivered them from the bitterness of the past. Even the skeptical had to admit they had seen a miracle. The impact of these changed lives triggered an explosion of repentance, restitution, and love.

Yet, the Derksen brothers could not have predicted what God was about to do. Even the most optimistic did not realize that this was the beginning of a revival that would affect thousands of people in Saskatoon and other cities in Canada. The movement popularly referred to as the "Canadian Revival" was on.*

---

*This page excerpted from Erwin W. Lutzer, *Flames of Freedom* (Chicago: Moody Press, 1976), 27–28. Used by permission.

attributes, namely, his eternal power and divine nature, have been clearly perceived, ever since the creation of the world, in the things that have been made. So they are without excuse.

Sin so distorts our discernment that we begin to think we can invent a god that will agree with us.

A high fever left nineteen-month-old Helen Keller without sight, hearing, and speech. But from age seven, she was blessed to have an excellent teacher in Anne Sullivan. Anne taught Helen how to communicate through touch. As they began to communicate, one of the first things Anne brought up to Helen was God. Young Helen said in sign language, "I already knew there was a God. I just didn't know His name."

The fool says in his heart, "There is no God" (Psalm 14:1). Creation shouts the existence of God. To say that creation was self-originating is against the law of cause and effect. Evolution is the greatest lie Satan has raised on the flagpole of human understanding. Even Darwin himself significantly regretted the things he had written by the end of his life (read the last page from The *Origin of Species*). The reason so many people cling with such tenacity to a theory that is very bad science is because they're suppressing the truth in unrighteousness.

Do you remember when Jonah was running from God? (Jonah 1). The sailors on the boat were frantic in the storm and came to Jonah with these words, "You better start praying to your God, man." Jonah confessed, "I worship the God of heaven and earth." And the sailors were like, "Oh. *That* God." They all knew. After Jonah went into the fish, they had a worship service. We're going to see the whole crew in heaven someday. Paul did the same thing in Acts 17:22–28 as he stood on the rocky hill that served as the sacred meeting place of the city's prime council. Listen to his argument for the existence of God:

> Men of Athens, I perceive that in every way you are very religious. For as I passed along and observed the objects of your worship, I found also an altar with this inscription, "To the unknown god." What therefore you worship as unknown, this I proclaim to you. The God who made the world and everything in it, being Lord of heaven and earth, does not live in temples made by man, nor is he served by human hands, as though he needed anything, since he himself gives to all mankind life and breath and everything. And he made from one man every nation of mankind to live on all the face of the earth, having determined allotted periods and the boundaries of their dwelling place, that they should seek God, in the hope that they might feel their way toward him and find him. Yet he is actually not far from each one of us, for "In him we live and move and have our being"; as even some of your own poets have said, "For we are indeed his offspring."

Romans 1 says that at the height of our sinful nature we suppress the reality of God's existence. Verse 20 says that we are without excuse. Literally, we have no defense. Have you ever pressed for a reason from a person who says he doesn't believe in God? He has no defense. Sin wants it to be true. Sin is shouting, "Ignore the truth, ignore your conscience, ignore the Creator." God has given every person on the face of the earth a chance to know the truth. We have no excuse.

Sin Is My Choice: It's Destroying My Mind

In the middle of verse 21 Paul says, **They became futile in their thinking.** Another word for *futile* is foolish or pointless; it's thinking that is soft or logically unsound. When sin drives the decisions, we can expect a lot of foolish thinking.

Here's what sin does:

Hey, isn't that wrong what you're doing there? "No, in my opinion this is what's best for me."

But doesn't the Bible say that's sin? "Well, it's what I want to be true now that's important. My opinion is what pleases me."

Why are you doing that? "So I'll be happy for the next few minutes."

What will it feel like after that? "I'm going to feel awful. Again."

Why do you keep doing that? "I don't know."

What's the problem? Futile thinking—not rigorous, not rooted in sound judgment. In fact, sin so distorts our discernment that we begin to think we can invent a god that will agree with us. Romans 1:22–23 summarizes, **Claiming to be wise, they became fools, and exchanged the glory of the immortal God for images resembling mortal man and birds and animals and reptiles.**

Everybody worships. If you don't worship the God of creation through His Son Jesus Christ, then you worship something else. The world is full of man-made religions, self-appointed, self-made, or substitute gods. To the sound-minded person, making up your own god is so insane it's silly; but to the mind darkened by sin, it's the natural next step. Notice the consequences of sin unchecked:

Romans 1:24 says, **Therefore *God gave them up* in the lusts of their hearts** (emphasis added).

Romans 1:26 says, **For this reason** *God gave them up* **to dishonorable passions** (emphasis added).

Romans 1:28 says, **And since they did not see fit to acknowledge God,** *God gave them up* (emphasis added). What does it mean that "God gave them up"?

Does God Really Give People Up to Sin?

Samson was a slave to sensual pleasure. Remember how Delilah tempted him with sexual sin as a way to learn the secret of his strength? Finally she shaved off the locks of his head and called out the enemy. Sampson met the Philistines at the door saying, **"I will go out as at other times and shake myself free." But he did not know that the LORD had left him** (Judges 16:20).

In fact, the Lord had departed from the whole nation of Israel in that dark time. In Judges 10, God had told them, **You have forsaken Me . . . Therefore I will deliver you no more. Go and cry out to the gods which you have chosen; let them deliver you in your time of distress** (vv. 13–14 NKJV). Their futile minds had so deteriorated because of sin that they had made up idols to take God's place. And God was saying in effect, "You think that's better than Me? You think that's going to meet your needs? Go have that and we'll see if your idols satisfy your hearts."

Proverbs 1:24–31 further details the consequences of choosing a pattern of sin.

Because I [God] have called and you refused to listen, have stretched out my hand and no one has heeded, because you have ignored all my counsel and would have none of my reproof, I also will laugh at your calamity; I will mock when terror strikes you,

when terror strikes you like a storm and your calamity comes like a whirlwind, when distress and anguish come upon you. Then they will call upon me, but I will not answer; they will seek me diligently but will not find me. Because they hated knowledge and did not choose the fear of the LORD, would have none of my counsel and despised all my reproof, therefore they shall eat the fruit of their way, and have their fill of their own devices.

These are the consequences of choosing sin after coming to faith. They are seldom preached on or talked about in this day of hyper-grace, but they are all too often experienced.

> *Grace easily turns to hyper-grace in a world that has lost its view of God's throne room and a biblical theology of sin.*

Hosea 4:17 echoes the consequence of unchecked sin in the life of a believer: **Ephraim [Israel] is joined to idols; leave him alone.** That's what God says. How many people does God look at today and say, "So-and-so is joined to idols; leave him alone"?

Jesus said this same thing in Matthew 15:14 regarding the Pharisees: **"Let them alone; they are blind guides. And if the blind lead the blind, both will fall into a pit."** They were left alone to the consequences of the sin they had chosen. We'd like to think that God will give us more time. But this idea that "I'll come back to God when I'm good and ready" is such foolishness. Grace easily turns to hyper-grace in a world that has lost its view of God's throne room and a biblical theology of sin.

It would be easy at this point to turn our attention to the sin in your mirror and begin by God's grace to remove it so your downpour will come. It is better though to remain for a few more pages in Romans 1 and make sure we have fully considered the consequences of lingering in sin. I want you to notice where sin takes a person. If you are in Christ, God would not allow you, nor would you desire to go down this road. But many people who think they are in Christ prove finally that they are not by making these choices. Keep reading and refresh your thinking on just how slippery the slope of sin actually is. Consider these four steps down:

Four Steps Down

1. Unrestrained Passion: "I want it even if it's wrong."

Romans 1:24 says, **Therefore God gave them up in the lusts of their hearts to impurity, to the dishonoring of their bodies among themselves, because they exchanged the truth about God for a lie.** That word *impurity* means "indecent acts that defile the body" and make the person unclean. "Dishonoring their body" describes anything for which we should be ashamed. Sadly, that's not where it ends.

2. Perversion: "I want the wrong even if it hurts me."

Romans 1:26 says, **For this reason God gave them up to dishonorable passions. For their women exchanged natural relations for those that are contrary to nature.**

You don't have to be a biologist to figure out the miraculous way God made a man and a woman to come together in the confines of marriage in an intimacy that is mutually satisfying and easily accomplished. That expression of marital intimacy is the way God created sex to be. **And the men likewise gave up natural relations with women and were consumed with passion for one another,** men committing shameless acts with men and receiving in themselves the due penalty for their error (v. 27). This describes an unstoppable, insatiable appetite for things that only shame, enslave, destroy, and blind us to that reality by our own sin.

I remember back in the 1980s when President Reagan ordered the attorney general's commission on pornography. James Dobson had been asked to be part of that study. The study concluded that there's something about sexual sin that escalates in intensity so that the user needs more and more perversion to gain the same amount of arousal. Unrestrained passion leads to perversion, which leads to pandemonium.

3. Pandemonium: "I want it even if it hurts others."

Romans 1:28 says, And since they did not see fit to acknowledge God, God gave them up to a debased mind to do what ought not to be done. They were filled with all manner of unrighteousness, evil, covetousness, malice. They are full of envy, murder, strife, deceit, maliciousness. They are gossips, slanderers, haters of God, insolent, haughty, boastful, inventors of evil, disobedient to parents, foolish, faithless, heartless, ruthless.

Sexual sin is only the first illustration of how wrong choices spiral out of control. Paul now adds many other sins to that list. These sins are often excused or ignored in our lives. But they bring shame and lost mental capacity, and they move from passion (what I want when I want it) to perversion (even if it hurts me) to pandemonium (even if it hurts others). Do you see anything familiar in this list?

- envy (wishing you had the position or prestige of another)
- murder (hating someone else from your heart)
- strife (causing and continuing relational hardship)

- deceit (giving a wrong impression on purpose)
- maliciousness (expending energy to injure others)
- gossip and slander (words that wound and separate people)
- insolence (rude and resolute in your refusal to be influenced)
- haughty or boastful (proud)
- disobedient to parents (how did that get on the list?)
- foolish (lost capacity to discern what is wise and best)
- faithless (unwilling to trust or even turn to God in tough times)
- heartless (cold and calculating in your callousness)
- ruthless (unfeeling in regard to the pain your actions cause others)

Whatever the sin that God wants to show you in the mirror, whatever He wants out of the way so that He can bring a great revival to your heart, whatever that sin is—it follows that same downward spiral from passion (what I want when I want it) to perversion (even if it hurts me) to pandemonium (even if it hurts others). The final step down is a full-on commitment to promote my sin.

4. Promotion of Sin

Ever see a gay pride parade or watch in dismay as promoters of abortion rights zealously advance their right to sin? Ever wonder how a person gets to such an awful place in total blackout blindness?

Romans 1:32 says, **Though they know God's decree that those who practice such things deserve to die, they not only do them but give approval to those who practice them.** When a person reaches this level, there is little hope they will ever come back. This is absolute rock bottom. He is in the grip of sin. When a person reaches this level of desperation, it usually concludes with self-destruction. Sin is ruthless, and Satan is a devourer.

Theology of Sin: In the Mirror

Now that we see afresh from God's Word where sin takes us, we should be ready to *run* in the other direction. To help us do that, I want to review in more detail the kinds of sins that too often remain lodged in the life of a believer. Let's get specific about sin in your life. Here are three broad categories that can help you begin to characterize the areas where you need God to work.

> *Pride is the complete state of anti-god. It's self-centered thinking.*

Pride. Hardly anyone would disagree that pride is sin. Pride is the complete state of anti-god. It's self-centered thinking— I, me, my, mine, me first, all the time, nobody else. Acting-like-I'm-better-than-I-am, have-others-notice-me, don't-make-me-look-bad-or-I'll-make-you-pay pride.

Pleasure. Pleasure itself is not sin because God **richly supplies us with all things to enjoy** (1 Timothy 6:17 NASB). Pleasure becomes sin when we pursue it at the wrong time, with the wrong person, or in the wrong amount.

Priorities. This group describes the good left undone. Do you know to love your neighbor, pay your bills, walk with God, tell others about Jesus, forgive when you are injured? Do you know to do these things? James 4:17 says, **Whoever knows the right thing to do and fails to do it, for him it is sin.**

Pride, pleasure, and priorities are just three broad categories of sin. If we want to see sin in the mirror, we have to drill down into a lot more detail. Can you handle it? This is the hard work so many people are not doing, and the result is the spiritual poverty we have come to call "normal." So let's go after this with energy and believe that an outpouring of blessing and favor from God Himself is the reward on the other side of this look at personal sin.

Under each of the three broad categories are three sub-categories of sin in that area. Beyond that is a countless list of specifics. Let's review the subcategories.

Pride	Pleasure	Priorities
Position	Sex	Self
Prestige	Substance	Others
Power	Stuff	God

Pride

Position. "Finally I have the corner office." "I can't believe you asked me to do this. Don't you know who I am?" "Nobody talks to me like that." "I haven't worked as hard as I have to put up with . . . ." I think you get the picture. It's thoughts of superiority in relation to others because of a role you have attained or a status you have achieved. It's the need to have your title mentioned or for everyone "under" you to salute as you pass. It can happen in the marketplace or even in your own home. It's the need to constantly remind others of who they are in relation to you.

Prestige. "More 'atta-boys' for me, please." "Tell me again how much you appreciate me and what I've done for you." "I want prizes and bonuses and thank-you notes and public acknowledgments." This is a consuming need for recognition. It's the feeling that others are always watching and the insatiable thirst for others to pat you on the back. It's the insistence that nothing you do be overlooked or unrewarded by those in a position to do so. It's dropping names of prestigious associations, it's letting others know of your accomplishments, it's the constant concern that everyone "knows who you are."

Power. "When I say, 'Jump,' you ask, 'How high?'" "You are my daughter and you'll do what I say." "I'm the boss—and don't you ever forget it." This is the inappropriate use of influence. It's throttling up over someone else and using your words, your position, or your persona to force them to do something against their best interest. Worse, it's reveling in and glorying in the ability to affect others that way. Inappropriate displays of power and the love of power is incredibly destructive sin, and it's something God despises to see in His children.

Pleasure

Sex. Not the good and the beautiful as God created but "my needs, what I want—when I want it. I don't care who it hurts. I don't care who it degrades. Everything for me." This sin is rampant and out of control in our world and is making serious headway even in the church. A startling number of pastors and Christian leaders admit to private sexual addiction. Like a bad cavity, it eats away at the core of what following Christ really is. It's sin.

Substance abuse. Beware of any substance (legal or not) that dulls your need for God. Why do people drink so much alcohol? Why do people take drugs—legally or illegally? "They kind of dull the edge for me," you might say. "They soften the pain of life and keep me from experiencing the hard things in my life."

Listen, God doesn't want the edge of life softened. God wants you to experience it full-on. That's what shows you how much you need Him. God wants to fill up what's lacking in your capacity to cope with life. The great wickedness of substance abuse is that it keeps you from seeing how much you really need God. It doesn't matter if you have to have sugar or Starbucks or cigarettes, God does not want you to be under the power of anything other than Him (see 1 Corinthians 6:12).

Stuff. It's not wrong to have things. It's wrong when things have you. Psalm 62:10b says, **If riches increase, set not your heart on them.** When my life is about wanting things and living for stuff, then I've got a sin problem. Don't let stuff be the source of your greatest joy or satisfaction. Stuff pursued in the wrong amount or at the wrong time or for the wrong reasons is sin.

Priorities

Priority of personal care. Sometimes sin is not taking care of yourself, personally. Are you doing what you can to be healthy? Do you realize that your body is not your own, but that you belong to God (1 Corinthians 6:19–20)? Overeating, failure to exercise, refusal to rest and relax as needed are all sinful choices that reflect a wrong priority in stewarding your life for God. You may have heard the foolish statement, "I'd rather burn out than rust out for God." As God's children we are required to care for this temple of the Holy Spirit, not in a preoccupied, consuming way but in a healthy, self-controlled way. To fail in time and health management is to leave the good undone, and that makes it sin. Do you need to confess it as such?

Priority of others. Do you make relationships a priority? How do you act when someone disappoints you or fails you? Are you becoming more loving? More forgiving? Kinder? More tender-hearted toward others (Ephesians 4:29–32)? This sin can be a failure to give ourselves to the people in our lives the way we should. Men, do we fail to open up and give ourselves to our wives in a way that is personally disclosing and relationally satisfying to them? To close up and withhold yourself from your spouse or your children or from anyone in your life who needs you and can rightfully claim your time is sin.

Failure to forgive is often at the root of failing to love. "But you don't know what they did to me," you might say. I don't need to know. God knows. Forgiveness is a choice to release a person from the obligation that resulted when they injured you. Failing to forgive that person before God is sin. **Be kind to one another, tenderhearted, forgiving one another, as God in Christ forgave you** (Ephesians 4:32). All failure to love and give myself and forgive those who injure me is failure to prioritize what matters to God—which is people. That failure is leaving that good priority undone, and it is sin.

Priority of your relationship with God. This is something only you can answer: Are you loving Christ with all of your heart, soul, mind, and strength? If you go to a worship service and just watch others, you are withholding yourself from God—it's sin.

Are you walking with God? You know that it's a good thing to spend time in prayer and Bible study every day, but are you doing that? If you know it's good and you don't do it—it's sin.

Only you can answer what categories are convicting you. Read over the list again and ask God to show you where you need to focus. He will. He desperately wants you to be free from sin and to move under the nourishing downpour of His favor. Sin can only be dealt with when we call it what it really is. Stop for a moment and say these words out loud, "It's sin." Say it again, "It's sin." Cultivate that discipline of calling your behavior that fails to keep God's law what it really is—it's sin.

Let's Review

In the first chapter, we looked at God on the throne, a picture of holiness. We discussed the importance of seeing God in His rightful place, high and lifted up. Only when we see God and His infinite standard of holiness do we begin to open our hearts to the reality of how far short all of us fall (Romans 3:23).

The purpose of this chapter has been to help us get low enough to see sin in the mirror. Nobody sees personal sin from "high on their horse." We have to get low to recognize the way sin is clogging the arteries of our relationship with God. We need to give God unlimited access, full permission to shine His light into every dark corner of our souls. Do the surgery, God. Get it all.

I urge you now to continue with the Activate, Elevate, and Replicate exercises.

ACTIVATE

Pray as you pull out your "mirror" and ask God to show you what is keeping your life dry and distant from Him. Ask Him to be specific in revealing what sin you need to see and confess.

A List of Specific Attitude Sins to Confess

1. We've learned that sin is both attitude and action. On the next page is a list of sins that includes things believers deal with every day. Place a number, from 0 to 10, before each item to indicate the extent of its presence in your life. Mark 0 if it is not an issue at all and 10 if it is a point of frequent failure in your life.

Go slowly, asking God for a total honesty and refusal to play games or pretend anymore. Are you with Him right now? Get on your knees and say, "Show me, God. I want this cancer removed, and I know that must begin with accurate diagnosis. Show me my sin as You see it and be as specific as You need to be. Help me to be honest with myself and before You."

_____Addiction	_____Feeling worthless	_____Prejudice
_____Anger	_____Gluttony	_____Profanity
_____Anxiety	_____Greediness	_____Projecting blame
_____Argumentative	_____Guilt (false)	_____Prone to gossip
_____Bigotry	_____Hatred	_____Rebellion to authority
_____Bitterness	_____Homosexual lust	_____Resentment
_____Boastful	_____Hostility	_____Restlessness
_____Bossiness	_____Idolatry	_____Sadness
_____Causing dissension	_____Impatience	_____Self-centeredness
_____Conceit	_____Impulsiveness	_____Self-confidence
_____Controlled by emotions	_____Impure thoughts	_____Self-gratification
_____Controlled by peer pressure	_____Indifferent to others	_____Self-hatred
	_____Inhibited	_____Self-indulgence
_____Covetousness	_____Insecurity	_____Self-justification
_____Critical tongue	_____Intemperance	_____Self-pity
_____Deceitfulness	_____Jealousy	_____Self-reliance
_____Depression	_____Laziness	_____Self-righteousness
_____Dominance	_____Loner	_____Self-sufficiency
_____Drug dependence	_____Lust for pleasure	_____Sensuality
_____Drunkenness	_____Materialistic	_____Sexual lust
_____Envy (depressed by the good fortune of others	_____Must repay kindness	_____Slow to forgive
	_____Negativism	_____Stubbornness
_____False modesty	_____Occult involvement	_____Temper
_____Fear	_____Opinionated	_____Unloving
_____Feeling helpless	_____Overly quiet	_____Vanity
_____Feeling rejected	_____Overly sensitive to criticism	_____Withdrawal
_____Feeling stupid		_____Workaholic
	_____Passivity	

2. In your journal or on a separate piece of paper, write a list of the sins that God is showing you. Make two columns. In the left column, describe the sin very specifically. In the right column, describe the consequences. What is the result of this specific sin? In you? In others? Add as many rows to your chart as you need. (One example is given to get you started on this exercise.)

My Sin	My Consequences
A critical tongue. "I speak critically and harshly to my husband when he doesn't measure up to what I think he should; I want to hurt him with my words."	*Our relationship stinks.* "My husband is distant and preoccupied with other things. He hasn't paid attention to me in months."

This is a very hard exercise, but you can't go on until you've completed it. You may need to return to this list several times before you have complete honesty before God on all points. Keep in mind that your "bigger sins" are the things that hang over your life like an umbrella, deflecting God's blessing. I have faith that you are really ready to deal with these things God's way. That's coming in the next chapter, but there is no point scouring your heart if you avoid the difficult corners.

Go back over the list again, and ask God to reveal to you any self-deception that may be clouding your capacity to see your true self in the mirror. If you want to make absolutely sure, go over the list in a prayerful way with a trusted friend. If you are blessed to have such a friend, he or she can help you with the blind spots where we simply cannot see ourselves as we really are.

What Should I Do with This New Understanding of My Sin?

1. Are you newly aware of sins in your life that you didn't recognize as sin before? As discouraging as this fresh exposure is, do you see how good it is? Your increased sensitivity to sin is a mark of a heart that God is reviving.

2. Feel the weight of your sin. Don't move too quickly to "fixing it." Be broken by it. Let the weight of your failure and its painful consequences in your life build genuine grief in you. Don't run from the pain of your own sin. Face it, and you'll be ready to deal with it in the next chapter.

3. You're going to be tempted to put this off for another day. But don't avoid this hard work. Don't be deceived into thinking that God will wait forever for you to get right with Him. Have you entertained the idea that "I'm not ready yet to deal with this stuff? I'll come back to God when I'm in a better place"? That's foolish thinking. Hebrews 4:7 says, **Today, if you hear his voice, do not harden your hearts.**

4. Don't go to bed tonight without doing this serious heart-work. Aren't you tired of carrying this burden around? Don't you want to be free of it? Don't you want all that God has planned for you?

5. Just do it! And you'll be ready for the downpour! The clouds are beginning to form even now.

ELEVATE

Lord, a few moments of honesty bring my sin quickly to mind. I see it. So do You. Let me see it in the same way You do—in all of its nastiness. I yield to You. I want a full understanding of the things that have kept my heart dry and at a distance from You. I see it all now—not just the "acceptable" sins, but the ones I've hidden and nurtured for years. Thank You for bringing them to light. I can't imagine my private life without this burden; but I'm here, right now in faith, asking that You take it all far away from me. No more covering. No more hiding. No more rationalizing. I believe that You are stirring a revival within me, and I know this dealing with sin has to come first. So I am coming in faith that You will help me. In Jesus' name. Amen.

REPLICATE

Next, get with a brother or sister in Christ very soon. James 5:16 says, **Confess your sins to one another.** Some churches wrongly think you need to confess your sins to one person in a supposed position of superiority, but all Christians are on equal footing before God. There are two good reasons to confess to one another.

1. To get it in the open. The apostle John wrote that confessing our sins gives us fellowship with others and forgiveness through Christ: **But if we walk in the light** [that is, get our sins out in the light where we can work on them] **as he is in the light, we have fellowship with one another, and the blood of Jesus his Son cleanses us from all sin** (1 John 1:7).

2. To get some prayer support. When someone who loves and supports you is aware of the sins that trip you up, he/she will become a faithful prayer supporter. Everyone wants to pray about things they know God is willing to do.

Be mutually committed to helping each other seek God's highest and best for your lives. That begins with this difficult step, but it continues in the joy of revival.

For even if I made you grieve with my letter,

I do not regret it—though I did regret it, for I see that

that letter grieved you, though only for a while.

As it is, I rejoice, not because you were grieved,

but because you were grieved into repenting.

For you felt a godly grief, so that you suffered no loss

through us. For godly grief produces a repentance that

leads to salvation without regret, whereas worldly grief

produces death. For see what earnestness this godly grief

has produced in you, but also what eagerness to clear

yourselves, what indignation, what fear, what longing,

what zeal, what punishment! At every point you have

proved yourselves innocent in the matter.

2 CORINTHIANS 7:8–11

CHAPTER 4

Self in the Dirt: A Picture of Repentance

I have to say I've been excited to get to this chapter with you. This is the chapter where we move from learning *about* downpour to *experiencing* it firsthand. If you do exactly what this chapter teaches, you will be under a downpour of mercy and joyfully laughing in the rain in the very near future.

The absolute essential thought in all of this is *repentance*. Repentance is the funnel through which all personal revival flows. Repentance is the natural next step on our journey. We have seen God's holiness exalted before our eyes. We have been brought to a place of personal brokenness about own sin and the tsunami of consequences that devastate our experience as the aftershock of personal sin. Repentance is the first step in a personal cleanup of the wreckage that sin brings. Refusing repentance only takes us down and never takes us up. Denial of sin only takes us backward and never forward. Repentance alone opens the way to a fresh outpouring of God's favor in our lives.

No wonder repentance is such a common theme in God's Word. Let's get into this study together.

Repentance Is a Good Thing

Trust me on this one; you want more repentance in your life. Though it's not an easy or pleasant thing, it is a good thing. If you want to get to a better place with God, get repentance.

The church at Corinth that Paul was writing to was the most problematic church in the New Testament. The people in this worldly church were filled with themselves; they were carnal and divisive. We know from studying the New Testament that Paul wrote four letters to the church at Corinth. Only two of them were ever found and declared as Scripture by the early church. In the letter we call 2 Corinthians, Paul pleaded with them to halt their sinful behavior. In 2 Corinthians Paul refers to an earlier corrective letter that he had written them: **For even if I made you grieve with my letter, I do not regret it.** Apparently the earlier letter was to the point, as in, "Hey, repent or else! I mean it, knock it off and repent or you're going to get it big time!"

Apparently, Paul had some moments of doubt about his strong rebuke because he said, **I did regret it.** Maybe he wondered to himself, "Did I say too much? Was I too hard on them?" Deep down, he knew that leading them to a place of grief over their sin was for their own benefit. It's good for us to feel sorrow over the wrong choices that we're making. It's right to feel grief over sin because that can lead us to some very important choices. You don't get to a better place with God until you recognize that where you are is not as good.

Sometimes you have to receive a hard word, something that you'd rather not hear, in order to get to the place you've always wanted to be. Paul felt that tension after he had written this strong, rebuking letter. Then he said, **I do not regret it—though I did regret it, for I see that that letter grieved you.** Apparently they were wounded by the truth, but it was only temporary. Eventually they repented, and that was the cause of Paul's rejoicing (v. 9).

Week after week I stand in the front of our worship center after service and pray with people, many of whom are grieving over their sin. In my heart I feel compassion for their pain, but I don't want to short-circuit what God is doing in their hearts. In my flesh I want to say, "It's O.K.; don't be so upset about what you've done." But I know they need to feel grief over

> *Repentance is the funnel through which all personal revival flows.*

sin in order to fully experience God's grace. Paul rejoiced because he knew that only when the Corinthian Christians were wounded by the reality of their sinful choices could they begin to experience the renewing power of His Spirit at work in their lives. Paul rejoiced, **not because you were grieved, but because you were grieved into repenting** (2 Corinthians 7:9).

The truth of these two difficult chapters, "Sin in the Mirror" and "Self in the Dirt," can lead each of us to a changed life through repentance. It's this life change that makes hearing the hard truth not only worthwhile but cause for rejoicing. No doubt about it, repentance is a very good thing.

Repentance is the moment when everything changes. God is not reluctant or unwilling to unleash a downpour of blessing upon your life. Even now, the clouds of heaven are bursting with the grace and mercy of God that will shower upon your parched heart at the moment of genuine repentance. Picture it now by faith: all of God's favor, all of God's grace, all of God's blessing, curling like a mighty wave and breaking upon the shore of your life. This comes only through repentance.

The Way It's Always Been

No wonder repentance was the method in the mouth of every biblical messenger. *Repent* was the one-word sermon from every Old Testament prophet. Isaiah, Jeremiah, Ezekiel, Hosea —all of them preached this one-word message. It was plagiarism to the max. They

> *You don't get to a better place with God until you recognize that where you are is not as good.*

would show up before a group of people and say, "Good morning . . . repent . . . let's pray." This method and message was fantastic in how it moved God's people.

Now in case you're thinking that was just an Old Testament thing, consider the prominence of repentance in the New Testament. Jesus said John the Baptist was the greatest prophet ever born to a woman. What was his message? **"Repent, for the kingdom of heaven is at hand"** (Matthew 3:2). Mark 6:12 says that Jesus sent them out and they went and **proclaimed that people should repent.** In fact, Luke 15:7 makes an amazing assertion that there's more joy in heaven over one sinner who repents than over ninety-nine other people who are like, "I'm kind of tired of reading about repentance, I think I'll lay down now and take a little nap."

So that was in the Gospels. Was it time yet for some variety? Nope. Directly after the Holy Spirit came, Peter's first message was, "Repent!" But then he delivered a new message in his second sermon, right? No. In Acts 3:19, Peter preached, **"Repent therefore, and turn again, that your sins may be blotted out, that times of refreshing may come from the presence of the Lord."**

Peter got it right, didn't he? We all are desperately in need of "times of refreshing from the Lord." Wouldn't you love a new, fresh experience with God? I know I get so tired of living on leftovers: "When I was in college, God did this." "When we were newly married, we saw God do amazing things in us." What about today? What about what God wants to do in your life—today? Repentance is the absolute essential that can bring those "times of refreshing."

"I didn't know repentance was that important," you might be saying. Acts 17:30 says, **The times of ignorance God overlooked, but now he commands all people everywhere to repent.** It's one thing if you didn't know that repentance was important. God can overlook that, but now that you know . . . .

Jesus and Repentance

You say, "Well, that's fine for the apostles, but that's not the tender heart of Jesus for me." In Revelation 2:5, Jesus says, **"Remember therefore from where you have fallen; repent."** Do you ever think, *I thought by now I'd be further along in my spiritual life; what should I do?* Do this: repent. Wake up to the reality that you're not progressing as you want to in your faith because there are some things that need to change in your life—and that happens through repentance. *My life was a mess until I found the Lord, and I was so close to Him for a while; but then I started to wander. What does He want me to do now?* Repent and return to the way you saw yourself and your sin and God's holy requirements when you first turned to Him.

This is the heart of Christ for the church today even if it takes drastic measures. In Revelation 2:16, the Lord says to the church, **"Therefore repent. If not, I will come to you soon and war against them with the sword of my mouth."** Jesus Christ Himself is moving today in resistance against every person who will not humble himself and repent of his sins. "That doesn't sound like the Jesus I hear preached about so often today," you may be saying. Too often Jesus is characterized like some overindulgent parent: "Of

course you can have whatever you want. Of course I'll answer your
prayers as soon as you think I should. Here, have another cup-
cake." Those are the words we put in the Savior's mouth, but now
hear what He really says: **"As many as I
love, I *rebuke and chasten*. Therefore be
zealous and repent"** (Revelation 3:19
NKJV, emphasis added).

*Repentance is
the moment when
everything changes.*

I don't know what your life has been
like. I don't know where you've been or what you've done. You
may have chosen some paths that you're not proud of, done some
things that you would be ashamed for others to know. Believe me
on this: God can and will wipe all that shame and sadness away
if you will only repent. **Come now, let us reason together, says
the LORD: though your sins are like scarlet, they shall be as
white as snow; though they are red like crimson, they shall
become like wool** (Isaiah 1:18). How can that happen? How can
you leave your past behind you? It's the bull's-eye of this whole
chapter: repentance.

Repentance Is Change Inside Me

Repentance is change in every way and at every level. Repentance is change in me—not a change of spouse, not a change of
job, or where I live or who I hang out with. Repentance is change
in the place where it's needed most—inside me.

If you study all the Hebrew and Greek terms together, you
get this three-part definition: repentance is a recognition of sin
for what it is, followed by a heartfelt sorrow, culminating in a
change of behavior. I see it for what it is (changing my mind). I
experience heartfelt sorrow (changing my heart). I determine to
change my behavior (changing my will). Repentance is change

From the Life of Jonah:
A Picture of Repentance

Jonah 1–3; Romans 2:2–4

Who doesn't love hearing testimonies about what God has done in people's lives? Just set up the microphones and get comfortable—we could listen all day.

That is, unless these people boasting of God's grace have hurt us, or worse, hurt the ones we love. What do we do when justice seems unseated and silent? Instead of listening and rejoicing over God's grace, it is then we bring down the judge's gavel. *Grace is too good for them.*

Such was the mind-set of Jonah that sent him on his infamous Mediterranean cruise. More than just disobedient, Jonah thought in some silly, small way that he could keep the kindness of God from reaching his enemies. Jonah had pronounced himself their judge, and no one could object—Nineveh didn't deserve God's mercy. But somewhere in the bowels of the fish, Jonah realized that he didn't either.

There in that protected, surreal, secret place, God finally got Jonah's attention. He could have let Jonah drown. He could have let him endure some second-rate life in Tarshish. But in His kindness, God went after full reversal. He put Jonah in a place where he would finally grieve his sin and recognize that he was to blame for his own wrong choices.

Now Jonah didn't think he was ever coming out of that fish. Read his prayer in Jonah 2 and you hear a man wrapping up the last moments of his life. Jonah thought, *I'm going to be standing before God in just a moment, so I'd better get right with Him now.* Jonah had no idea what God had prepared to do the moment he repented.

So it didn't take long for the spit-up, bleached-out, "poster-boy of the second chance" to get on the road to Nineveh once his heart had returned to God. As he had promised, Jonah proclaimed God's great salvation to the people he loathed and watched God rain a downpour of mercy on the wicked. Jonah's call to "repent-or else" coursed like a mighty river through the streets of the vast city. And as Jonah preached doom, the people understood the righteous anger of a holy God, turned from their horrific ways, and repented in sackcloth and ashes. From the greatest to the least, the people of Nineveh threw themselves on God's mercy. And God heard their cry.

With the same outrageous grace that spared Jonah, God now spared Nineveh. His kindness drew them to repentance, and God's mercy overruled revenge. As hearts were revived, they recognized their sin for what it was and humbled themselves under God's mighty hand. And to no one's surprise, God stepped toward them with open arms.

at every level of your being—in your mind, your emotions, and your will.

The prodigal son is the poster-boy for repentance. It's all in Luke 15. There was this know-it-all kid who came up with a rebellious plan. He demanded of his father all the money from his inheritance in order to live the life of his dreams. Apparently the father was permissive because he did what the son asked. Then according to Luke 15:13, the son **squandered his property in reckless living.** He was a party animal, and he ended up living with the animals. One day he was so hungry he craved the pigs' food. The life of his dreams?—more like a nightmare.

> *God can and will wipe all that shame and sadness away if you will only repent.*

Then he woke up (the first step). Luke 15:17 says, **He came to himself** or "came to his senses." He recognized the sin in his life for what it was—that is the first step to repentance: changing your mind about sin. Next he said, **I am no longer worthy to be called your son** (v. 19). He felt shame over his action and more like a slave than a son. That's changing his heart about sin (second step). Then the prodigal son said, **I will arise and go to my father, and I will say to him** (v. 18). That's a change of his will, resulting in a change of behavior (third step).

That son who a short time before thought sin was so attractive, and who felt a right to whatever satisfaction he craved no matter who it hurt, and who couldn't wait to get as far as possible from his family, *that son* repented and everything changed. His thoughts changed, his feelings changed, his actions changed.

Repentance involves your mind (recognition of sin); your emotions (heartfelt sorrow); and your will (producing a specific plan of action for change).

Repentance before Revival

You've read four chapters so far in this book, so I know you're serious about getting on a fresh page with God. But here's the truth: you can agree that you need a downpour of His blessing, but still not experience it. Why? Because we fail at this point of repentance.

You want more of God's grace? He longs to give it to you, but it's not coming until you put away your sin. More of God's presence and power and peace?—absolutely! But not without a pure heart.

Repentance involves your mind, your emotions, and your will.

God's greatest blessings are yours, but not without a turning. The days of hyper-grace are over. We must come back to biblical Christianity where true, transforming grace flows to the place of heartfelt repentance.

I'm going to hang on here for just a moment and share with you how this is impacting me. I told you in the last chapter that we each needed to have a personal time of confessing our sin to one another. In between writing these two chapters, I met with one of our elders for breakfast and confessed some sin to him—some sin in my life that I had allowed to linger too long. I confessed to him some action sins, some attitude sins, and some things that I don't want to finish my life still dragging behind me. I don't want to be like, "I know I should have repented in that area, Lord. Sorry, I just never got around to it."

I want God to get it all, don't you? I want to become totally pure and holy before God, and I have to confess I've still got room to grow. But I'm making progress, and by God's grace you are, too, right?

Ready to Get It Done?

If you are reading carefully and working hard at the application exercises, you should be holding in your hands some specific sins you've seen in the mirror of God's holiness. You are convinced of the need to repent in order to experience a fresh downpour of God's grace. Are you there? If not, circle back. There's no point in reading further if your mind is filled only with generic intentions and vague objectives. This truth has not yet moved from your head to your heart.

> I don't want an "A" for appearance—I want the real thing in my heart. I don't want to look right—I want to be right.

Remember that your target is personal revival. The barrier to that goal is your personal sin in the eyes of a holy God. Your heart is crying out for a clean heart, but God's grace does not reach generalities. Are you ready to repent of specific sin and see yourself in the dirt? Put a marker in this page and go back and reread chapter 3 or revisit the exercises at the end of "Sin in the Mirror."

Spend private, intimate time with the Lord on this subject of your specific sin. I told you that this repentance thing would not be easy, but there's no going forward unless we do it right. And don't put off this step or you'll soon be lost in that barren wasteland again—dry and distant from God. Go do your part now, and come back when you're ready for God to do His work. Are you with me?

It's Now or Never

If it seems like I am dragging here a bit, it's because I am. I realize that many of you are ready to get to work on repentance, but there are surely some stubborn sheep who want to linger in the lowlands a little longer. Those of you who are ready to repent, let's move on together; those of you who are not quite ready, I'm sorry but this is where we leave you behind.

Why So Low?

All through the Old Testament we meet people who, when they truly repented, would put on sackcloth. Picture a big potato sack with holes for your head and arms with a piece of bailing string that cinched it together at your waist. Would you ever come to church like that? People did in Old Testament times. Of course when people saw them they knew: "Whoa, guess you're going through some serious soul-searching."

The whole point of sackcloth was a radical rejection of externals. Taking off their fine clothes they would wear sacks instead. Then they would take ashes out of the fire bed and smear the soot on their faces and throw it over their heads, allowing it to cover them in "funeral gray." In effect they were saying, "I don't care about looking the part anymore. I don't want an 'A' for appearance— I want the real thing in my heart. I don't want to *look* right—I want to *be* right. I don't want to *appear* to be right with God, I want to *be* right with God, and I don't care what it takes. I'm done with posing and posturing. I don't want to arrive at church in my Sunday best and look good for the crowd; nothing phony anymore, not in my life. I'm going after the real thing."

Repentance Is a Work of God

At the end of this chapter you will find some specific exercises to help you in the crisis of repentance. There are some sparks to start the fire of your repentant conversation with God. What you won't find are "Five Easy Steps to Repentance" or "Thirty Days to a More Repentant You." Only God can give you a repentant heart. In fact, 2 Timothy 2:25 says, **God may perhaps *grant* them repentance** (emphasis added). Repentance is a gift that God gives to a person who wholeheartedly seeks Him. Maybe as you've been reading you've said to yourself, "But I don't feel grief over my sin." God will help you with that if you ask Him. Maybe you even believe your actions or attitudes are not wrong even though God's Word says they are. Again, what you desperately need is to seek God and ask Him to change your mind about that.

All in all, repentance is not easy. If it were, everyone would do it. Instead we have a worldly church struggling to build the kingdom in its own strength and failing miserably at its primary job—to display the power and glory of Jesus Christ. Too many impressive churches don't impress lost people with the impressiveness of all that Jesus is and longs to be for them.

Only God can grant us repentance about all that we have done and failed to do. I don't have any quick fixes to give you here. However, I can tell you how to know for sure that genuine repentance has taken place in your life.

How to Recognize Repentance

If we could hang out together for an extended time, I would know if you were repentant and you would know the same of me. There are marks or distinguishing characteristics in the behavior of a person who truly repents. I write this not on my own authority but on the authority of God's Word.

These marks are called "fruits of repentance." Acts 26:20 qualifies them as deeds appropriate to repentance: **"Repent and turn to God, performing deeds in keeping with their repentance."**

Luke 3:8 says, **"Bear fruits in keeping with repentance."** If you are repentant, others will be able to see it in your life. Your actions will show your heart. Repentance is the unseen, underground root that will eventually produce fruit in your life that will be apparent to everyone—including you. What are these fruits of repentance? Paul lists them in 2 Corinthians 7. If you remember, Paul had previously written that confrontational letter about their sin and now is able to joyfully report their repentant response and the fruit that their repentance is producing. In fact, in 2 Corinthians 7:9–11, Paul lists these fruits of Corinthian repentance. He's so fired up about their response that they come out kind of randomly. I understand why.

Enthusiasm vs. Organizational Excellence

The number of options at a grocery store and my proven tendency to fill the cart with Krispy Kremes and ice cream made it clear early in our marriage that my wife, Kathy, was the best one to buy the groceries. But when I go out to the garage to help Kathy unload, what do you think is the first thing I want to know? "What'd you get?" When she answers the question, she doesn't pour it out in perfect sequence. She might say, "I got some apples and stuff for lasagna, and some treats for the kids' lunches." She gives me the highlights. She doesn't give it to me systematically in the four food groups. She reports whatever comes to mind.

That's what Paul is doing when he reports the evidence of the Corinthians' repentance. He didn't lay out a perfectly arranged inventory of the fruits of repentance. He didn't detail the deeds from first to last or biggest to smallest. He just pours them out randomly and with great enthusiasm. He says in effect, "It fires me up to see the fruits of repentance like this and this and this"—and out it comes.

Paul lists eleven fruits in random order. But for our study I've grouped them here under five headings and in the order I believe a repentant person experiences them. So here they are, not as an enthusiastic grocery list, but sequentially as they occur in your life after true repentance.

Five Marks of Genuine Repentance

1. Grief over Sin

It's kind of hard to miss that in the text. Paul says in 2 Corinthians 7:9, **For you felt a godly grief,** then again in verse 10, **Godly grief produces a repentance that leads to** salvation. The word *grief* is the Greek word *lupeo*. It's the "greatly distressed" feeling the disciples had when Jesus announced His crucifixion in Matthew 17:23. This word for grief or sorrow is used twenty-six times in the New Testament. Half of those occurrences are in 2 Corinthians, with half of them right here in this passage. That fact makes this passage the most concentrated statement in all of Scripture about the feelings that accompany repentance.

If you're really repentant, you're going to feel some things. You'll feel grief over sin; you will feel "internal hurting, soul anguish." When you're convicted of sin and you repent of it, you will feel grief and shame about the wrong choice you made.

There was a college professor who used to come to our church. He doesn't come anymore because he said, "When I go there, I feel like a worm." I was sad about his decision, and I was sad to hear about his "worm feelings," but I wasn't sad that our church made him face his sin.

We need a lot more sin in the mirror at church. When you see the exalted holiness of God and your own sin in that mirror, you should start to lose your grip on "I have it totally together." Sometimes we need to feel like a worm and recognize our sin for what it is. This lack of genuinely facing our sin is reflected in the modern hymn books. They edit out the words "that saved a wretch like me" from *Amazing Grace,* and the words "for such a worm as I" out of *At the Cross.* This, of course, is symptomatic of our stubborn desire to avoid the truth about our own sin. This sort of "Oh, pastor, please make me feel as good as I am" Christianity has got to go. If we're going to go higher, we've got to go lower. If we want more of God and His transforming power, we have to begin with some honesty about the way we are living.

It's interesting that in Scripture people who make real contact with God do feel low, like a worm. Here are a few examples.

Abraham. When Abraham spoke to God about the wickedness of Sodom and Gomorrah, he discovered that God had some comments of His own. In response, Abraham could only say, **"I . . . am but dust and ashes"** (Genesis 18:27). When you really connect with God, you understand that God is everything and we're not that much.

Job. Job was a righteous man by any human standard. When he met with God, he said, **"I despise myself, and repent in dust and ashes"** (Job 42:6). The revealed nature of God showed Job how far he was falling short of holiness.

Isaiah. Remember when Isaiah saw God on the throne? He could only fall on his face and say, **"Woe is me . . . I am a man of unclean lips"** (Isaiah 6:5). That sense of unworthiness—or let's call it wormliness—is the immediate result of meeting with God. If you go to church and only feel puffed up about your current state of holiness, have you really met with God? Have you really seen His standard? God's standard of unattainable, infinite holiness reveals that even the most righteous among us is not coming close.

When Jesus revealed His glory through the miraculous catch of fish, Peter cowered before the omnipotent Christ and said, **"Depart from me, for I am a sinful man, O Lord"** (Luke 5:8). The Gentiles saw the power of Christ over the demoniac, and in their fear they pleaded with Jesus to leave them (Mark 5:17). John was in the Spirit, and when he saw the Lord he **fell at his feet as though dead** (Revelation 1:17). That's what it means to meet with God.

Real contact with God produces a sense of immense unworthiness.

Real contact with God produces a sense of immense unworthiness. When we see even a glimpse of God as He is, we feel in our hearts, "Whoa—the standard is high and I'm not making it." Soul anguish is not a bad thing, and heartfelt grief over sin is the first mark of true repentance.

True repentance is heartfelt sadness about what I've done to God. At the heart of every choice to sin is a rejection of God, and that's why the grief of repentance must begin with how my actions affect the Lord. When I choose the wrong, I'm really saying, "You're not enough, God. I need this too. You have not met my needs, so I'm going out on my own this time."

Repentance is happening in your heart when you begin to express through your grief, "How can I spit in the face of mercy? How can I slap away the hand of God's grace? God reaches out to bless me, and I shun His merciful love."

Repentance is detecting the lie that aided my sinful choice and destroying it. Repentance is grief over that lie I told myself and the choice I made because of it. Repentance shows up in my wounded spirit. *How could I have acted that way toward God? How could I treat His love so poorly when He's given me so much?* Real repentance recognizes that my sin is against God.

Think back to the chart on page 102 in chapter 3. Consider the categories of pride, pleasure, and priorities. Do you feel grief over anything in those categories? Will you allow God's Spirit to bring you to a place of heartfelt grief about specific patterns in your life?

When Grief Is No Good

Sometimes grief over sin is not recognized by God because it is not genuine. Too often our grief is only about the fix we're in. Some translations of this passage call it a worldly sorrow (2 Corinthians 7:10). In this scenario, you see your sin but grieve only the consequences. It's what the rich young ruler felt when Jesus told him to sell everything and follow Him in Matthew 19:22. The shallowness of his grief was revealed as he said in effect, "I'm sorry that You're requiring so much. I'm sorry that I can't do that." Examine your own sorrow over sin. Is it a worldly sorrow as in, "I'm sorry I feel so bad. I'm sorry I got caught. I'm sorry I don't look good in this. I'm sorry I'm not all You want me to be. I'm sorry I'm..." That's worldly sorrow—and it will never bring a downpour of God's blessing to your life.

If you can't, then you're not repenting. Without repentance there will never be a downpour of God's awesome presence in your life—not under any circumstances. It just won't come without repentance.

Whatever it is that holds you back from this downpour, bring it to God right now and sincerely ask for the heartfelt grief that He requires. You won't have to wait long to receive it. Sincerely ask, "Lord, show me my sin" or "Reveal to me how You see my sin" or "Bring me to the place where I experience Your sorrow over my sin." God has answered these kinds of requests quickly and abundantly in my life.

As you hold that grief in your hand, seeing the sin as God sees it, the second mark of true repentance follows quickly.

2. Repulsion over My Sin

Grief over sin leads very quickly to feelings of repulsion about that sin. Notice Paul says in verse 11: **For see what earnestness this godly grief has produced in you.** That word *see* means "to behold." The word *earnestness* implies diligence.

When I'm really repentant, I have serious energy about putting sin behind me. Repentance brings with it a new urgency about my relationship with God and strong negative feelings toward anything that would injure it. What used to be so attractive to me now repulses me. I'm indignant about it; I'm strongly opposed to it and resolutely determined that it will always be repulsive in my eyes.

A television program that I've caught a couple of times but now avoid is *Fear Factor*. The first part has all these cool competitions and extreme challenges, but the second part totally repulses me. That's when the contestants wallow in and even eat all these disgusting things. I'll tell you the truth—it's not entertaining; it's repulsive. It is only the basest part of us that would enjoy watching people swallow maggots or animal organs or whatever. That's an illustration of what repulsion feels like.

Repentance is when we feel that way about our sin. You look at what you used to do and go, "Bleecckkk, yuck!" It makes you gag to think of what you once thought could bring you joy. "I don't want to act like that anymore," you say. "I don't want to say those things. I'm tired of being a gossip. I'm so weary of my silly sensitivity and hurt feelings over every little perceived slight from everyone. When will I grow up and put that behind me once and for all?" Repentance is when whatever private satisfaction a specific sin brought me now makes me want to vomit because I see it for what it really is.

What specific sins from the Sin in the Mirror chart (page 107 in chapter 3) repulse you? Those broad categories of Pride, Pleasure, and Priorities are a good place to start. Are you sickened that every time you're in conversation you have to bring up your accomplishments? Do you name-drop? Do you later privately compare the ways you are better than someone else (pride)? Are there things on that list that are injuring your life in God (pleasure)? Do you feel grief about them? Do you regard your relationship with your spouse or with God as a lesser priority that His Word demands (priorities)? Will you let God's Spirit bring you to a place of repulsion about that?

Grief and repulsion about personal sin are the first two marks of genuine repentance.

Repentance Is Not a Solo Sport

God is the one who grants repentance, and you can't get it without Him.

John 3:21: Repentance is a deed **wrought in God** (NASB).

Acts 5:31: **God exalted [Jesus] . . . as Savior, to give repentance.**

Acts 11:18: **Then to the Gentiles also God has granted repentance.**

2 Timothy 2:25: **God may perhaps grant them repentance.**

As hard as you may try, you can't do the work of repentance in your own strength. You *can* seek the Lord and ask God to give you grief over sin. *Show me what it really is, God. Show it to me in all of its ugliness and cause me to be repulsed by it, Lord. I don't want that in my life anymore.*

3. Restitution toward Others

When repentance is happening in your heart, you will have an immediate and urgent desire to get to the people whom your sin has wounded and fix the fall-out. Repentance is when you don't just want to be right with God; you want to be reconciled to the people whom your sin has injured. It's a fruit of repentance. Some Bible translations call this **avenging of wrong** (NASB) and **readiness to see justice done** (NIV).

Zacchaeus is famous for this. As a tax collector, he was in a position to steal whatever he could get from everyone he worked with. When he repented, the first action he took was to make things right with those whom his sin had injured. "Man, this money doesn't belong to me," he said. "I've got to give it back. I don't want this at my house" (see Luke 19). Restitution is a

Evan Roberts Sparked Revival in Wales (1904)

The deacon at Evan Roberts's church probably didn't realize the fire that he stoked in teenager Evan's heart would eventually set their country of Wales ablaze with a passion for God. By the time he was twenty-six, Evan had been praying for revival—in his own life and in his country—for over a decade. Yet even in his diligence, Evan recognized a hardness in his heart. Evan once heard someone pray, "Lord, bend us," and knew immediately that this was his need. The next night in a prayer meeting, he knelt and cried out to the Lord, "Bend me! Bend me!"—and God did.

From that day forward, his life was ablaze with a love for God and the love of God for his countrymen. He and his friends began asking God for one hundred thousand souls to come to salvation. On Monday night, October 31, 1904, Evans brought this four-point message to his home church at Loughor, Wales:

1. Is there any sin in your past that you have not confessed to God? On your knees at once. Your past must be put away, and yourself cleansed.
2. Is there anything in your life that is doubtful—anything that you cannot decide whether it is good or evil? Away with it. There must not be a cloud between you and God.
3. Do what the Holy Spirit prompts you to do. Obey promptly, implicitly, and with unquestioning submission to God's Spirit.
4. Publicly profess Christ as your Savior.

His cry became, "Bend the church and save the world." Once again, God answered his prayer. As a matter of public record in 1904, sinful habits began to wane in Wales. Taverns closed, gambling businesses lost their trade, and brothels locked their doors. Families were reunited, broken friendships reconciled, profanity ceased, old debts were paid, stolen goods returned, forgiveness for past offenses flowed. Divisions in churches were healed, denominational and class barriers were broken down, feuds were forgotten, discord and enmity were replaced by peace and harmony and unity.

On that first night of Evan Roberts's preaching ministry, sixteen young people confessed Christ. The next night seven turned to Christ, and the third night, twenty people received Jesus Christ as Lord. Attendance at meetings began to grow and spread to other towns and villages. Names of converts were sent to the newspapers. After two months seventy thousand had come to Christ. By the end of March 1905, eighty-five thousand and ultimately one hundred thousand confessed faith in Jesus Christ.

A song that churches sang in 1905 echoed Roberts's prayer for revival: "Bend me lower, lower down at Jesus' feet." God used this young man to change the spiritual course of an entire generation in the country of Wales.*

*"Bend the Church and Save the World," vol. 18, no. 1, special edition of *Spirit of Revival* (Buchanan, MI: Life Action Ministries).

mark of genuine repentance. That's why Paul says, **What eagerness to clear yourselves.** That word *eagerness* in Greek is *apogolia*. It's the idea from which we get "apologetics," which means to give an explanation or reason. Restitution involves going to a person and saying, "What I did or said to you was wrong. I'm truly sorry I did that. I don't have any excuses. Will you forgive me?"

Repentance doesn't demand anything, but it does request reconciliation. Repentance admits being the reason for the separation in the first place. Repentance is no longer concerned with the other person's part of the problem—there's already been enough blame shifting—but confesses that *I* haven't been what *I'm* supposed to be so I'll make it right as much as I can and leave the rest with God. Repentance is doing what I need to do and what I can do.

"Yeah, well," you may say, "you don't know my spouse." No, I don't. But you can't fix that person. Even when you believe your responsibility is the smallest part, you need to be ready and willing to make it right. Repentance is immediately concerned about the people your sin has injured. That's why Paul says, **What earnestness . . . what eagerness to clear yourselves,** then in verse 11, **At every point you have proved yourself innocent in the matter.** *Innocent* means free of guilt, blameless in the eyes of others. You deal with your sin before the people whom your sin injured. Your spouse, your children, your boss, your neighbor, your faithful friend—all of these people now gladly report that you have done what you can to restore the fall-out your sin caused between you and them.

As you look in the rearview mirror of your life, maybe you've said or done some things that if others knew, you would feel incredibly ashamed. Maybe you carry those memories like a ten-ton weight on your back. Good news—that weight can be lifted! Through repentance, you can experience God's incredible grace and all-consuming forgiveness. You can break the chains to your past and you can go forward into a glorious future—but it does involve restitution. Large or small, you can be cleansed, you can be forgiven, you can be on a new, clean page under the grace of God. But you have to go all the way in repentance—which means restitution.

Many people want to be right with God, but they draw the line on being right with others. Watch out for the people who say that all is good between them and God but have no interest in being reconciled with the people whom their sin has injured. If your heart is really repentant and you see sin for what it is, you see not only how it affects God but how it impacts others.

> Watch out for the people who say that all is good between them and God but have no interest in being reconciled with the people whom their sin has injured.

I'm always burdened about the people who devastate their families and then say, "Yeah, I've got a new thing going with God." Have you talked to your family about it? If you were really repentant, you would make a beeline to the people who were devastated by the very choices that you are now repenting of. Go back to your parents, call your sister on the phone, write your old boss a letter, and tell them, "I'm sorry, I was wrong."

Restitution, when seriously contemplated, can raise some fear in our hearts. *What if they don't say anything? What if they tell me to get off their front porch?* Yes, you run the risk of them rejecting you, but then you will have done everything you know to do and you can leave their reaction with God. Do the best you can to build the bridge of reconciliation. No more excuses. No more blame-shifting. Take the responsibility for restitution. Go straight to that person and do all you can to make it right.

Repentance—mind, emotions, and will. No more rationalizing, no more excusing, no more blaming others. If that's really happening in your life, there will be grief over your sin, there will be repulsion, and there will be restitution.

4. Revival toward God

Like a river rushing down a mountainside, like a waterfall from a cool stream, God's mercy will now begin to wash over your life. Repentance will bring an obvious restoration of your relationship with the Lord. Your heart will become very sensitive to sin, and you will experience an increased capacity to rejoice in the blessings of God. You'll hunger more after God's Word and have less craving for things of the flesh. Paul points this out as he continues his grocery list of repentance results.

Paul characterizes the Corinthians' renewed relationship with God in the words, **What fear** (v. 11). Previously the Corinthians were involved in all kinds of sexual sin, and they didn't care what God thought. Their genuine repentance had increased in them "the fear of the Lord."

Fear is the attitude of heart that seeks a right relationship to the fear source. If I'm afraid of fire, I stand back a bit. If I'm afraid of water, I don't go in over my head. If I fear God, I'm very careful to do exactly as He asks, as quickly as I can. Fear of God is a good thing. **The fear of the LORD is the beginning of wisdom,** says Proverbs 9:10. Remember the thief on the cross who condemned the other thief for insulting Christ as He hung between them: **"Do you not fear God?"** (Luke 23:40). Every revived heart has an increased sense of God's nearness and our accountability to Him. The biblical term for that increased awe or respect is *fear*, and Paul observed that in the repentant Corinthians.

Paul also observed the revival flowing from their repentant hearts as an increased passion for the things of the Lord. He marveled, **What longing!** (v. 11). All of a sudden, church isn't a chore anymore for the repentant person. Bible study is not a burden. You delight in all that God and His people and His Word have for you.

Revival brings more of God in your life, experienced and enjoyed.

As an outgrowth of your repentance you might report, "I used to be so caught up in my problems and my burdens and anxiety about the future." Now instead the joy of the Lord has returned and you're excited about sharing your faith; you're looking forward to heaven. **What fear, what longing, what zeal,** Paul says in verse 11.

Zeal in the revived heart is an increased passion for the overall things of God. Life is not drudgery anymore. It doesn't matter what's in the newspaper this week or what's coming around the next corner. The revived person finds joy in every situation because he remembers this thing called *life* is only temporary. We're going to heaven someday! And until then, each breath is for God. This joy is a big part of revival. Remember our definition? Revival is *renewed interest after a period of indifference or decline*. Revival brings more of God in your life, experienced and enjoyed.

This is the place not many people know to go. Spiritually speaking, this is the road less traveled. But you can go. If you do, others will begin to observe in you, "What longing after God!"

5. Moving Forward

Here's the final mark of genuine repentance: moving forward and not looking back. So many people spend their lives lamenting what they see in the rearview mirror. If you're thinking, *Oh, if I would have chosen differently when I was in college. If only I had not, . . .*

If I had just quit, . . . If I hadn't gone there, . . . Why did I do that? Why am I like this? So many people have their lives sadly submerged in a sea of regret: What might have been . . . . It's easy to spot people who haven't repented—they live in the past. They're stuck. Everyday is about reviewing a series of tragic circumstances that lock their focus on what is already done. I hope this doesn't describe you.

Notice that genuine repentance eliminates that persistent regret: **Godly grief produces a repentance . . . without regret** (v. 10). When repentance is genuine, the human heart experiences cleansing; and by God's grace, it moves beyond the kind of self-punishment that's stuck in the past and can't or won't move into the future. You know repentance is truly happening in your heart when you get locked in on what's ahead and experience freedom from what's behind.

That's why Paul says in verse 9, **So that you suffered no loss through us.** Repentance never takes you to a bad place. Repentance is never a waste of time; it is never a shortfall or a write-off; it's not a ceaseless cycle of worldly regret. Paul reminded the Corinthians that repentance was not a loss to them but actually a gain because it got them out of the rut of a self-condemning past and moved them forward into the freshness of a revived relationship with God. *Today is the first day of the rest of my life.* When you can say that and mean it from your heart, it's a fruit of repentance.

Notice that **worldly grief produces death.** A lifetime of worldly repentance produces separation from God and hell for all of eternity. You can't have shallow repentance and pretend that you have God too. Your heart must have true repentance. You'll know that your repentance is true if you have grief over sin, repulsion over sin, restitution toward others, revival toward God, and if you're moving forward into a life that is free from regret.

O.K., that's it. I can't say any more about holiness, sin, and repentance. The ball is in your court now. All the information is on the table and available for your active embrace. Take some time now and move into an actual expression of repentance regarding the sin God has shown you in the mirror of your own life. If you do that now, with all your energy, the raindrops of restoration and revival will begin to fall upon you. By faith, I see the clouds of mercy forming. Now go for it!

ACTIVATE

Do you want revival? It all begins here. Radical change calls for a radical response. In this chapter, we explored five marks of genuine repentance. Let's make them personal.

Mark 1. Grief over Sin

1. Get your list of personal sins that God showed you "in the mirror" as you completed chapter 3.

2. Go to God with this list. Tell Him (or copy this into your journal), "Lord, I'm so sorry for this sin of _____ (be very specific). I confess this to You as sin; I say it out loud: _____ *is sin*. I have been excusing _____ in my life with the reasoning that _____ made it justifiable. I used to think I was pretty good, that I just needed some minor adjustments. Now I see _____. I now reverse those rationalizations by honestly confessing that You have been right all along. _____ is sin and I have no excuse. I bring it into the light of Your truth; and as I hold this sin of _____ in my hand, I feel _____. I'm so sorry, Lord, and I humbly ask Your forgiveness. Help me as I turn from this sin."

Mark 2. Repulsion over My Sin

3. Continue in your journal: "When I think about how I allowed this sin in my life for so long, I feel _____. This sin used to be so attractive but now my feelings are _____ ___. My perspective on this sin has changed from _____ ____ to _____."

Let's look again at the chart that appeared on page 102 in chapter 3. How does it make you feel to observe these sins in your life?

Pride	Pleasure	Priorities
Position	Sex	Self
Prestige	Substance	Others
Power	Stuff	God

Describe the specific ways you've personalized these sins. Write it out so you can see it for what it is. Example: "I privately compare the ways that I am better than someone else. Lord, this is pride and it makes me sick. By Your grace I want it out of my life."

Go over your list and allow God to give you feelings of repulsion about each one. Look into the heart of what a certain sin promises versus what it delivers. Reflect upon how this sin has damaged your relationship with God and others. Invite God's Spirit to give you a holy loathing about that sin. Write your thoughts here: _____

_____

_____

_____

_____

_____

ELEVATE

Lord, thank You for changing my heart. You have produced such a deep grief in me over what I've done. I have excused the inexcusable and blamed others for that which I'm responsible. I see that as sin now, and I'm turning around. As best as I know how, I'm repenting of all the things that have kept me dry and distant from You. It makes me sick just to think of how I've allowed this to linger in my life.

But by Your grace I am dealing with it now. Already I sense that You are welling up in me the hope of restoration and the rightness of reconciliation to You. Don't stop, Lord! I am stepping out in faith, performing deeds in keeping with repentance. Thank You for this renewed season of mercy to get this work done. I'm getting on the right road and I'm not looking back. This I pray in Jesus' name. Amen.

REPLICATE

Mark 3. Restitution toward Others

The best way to impact the lives of others is to make things right with those whom your sin has injured. That work is called restitution. Let me be totally transparent and tell you it will be the hardest part of this book for most who read it. But it will also produce the most genuine and lasting parts of personal revival.

Keep in mind that you are not alone in this. Here are just two of the many stories we hear from people who are putting into practice the same things you are now considering:

> "When I first heard about the link between restitution and repentance, God immediately brought four situations to my mind that I needed to make right. Driving home from church, I felt such a burden to get this work done as soon as I could, but it was too late in the day to call people. I determined that I would make contact with them first thing in the morning. I fell asleep figuring out what I needed to say. I was so excited, first that God was alive in me pointing out the areas where I needed to change, and

second, excited with hope that these relationships, broken or strained for so long, would be restored to health.

"But as I drove in to work the next morning, thinking through all that needed to be accomplished that day, I remembered these four phone calls that I was so impassioned to make the night before. From nowhere crept this thought, *Why was I feeling so urgent about this? Do it another day when you're not so busy.* GASP! Wherever that thought came from—either from the Evil One or from my own flesh—it *did not* come from God. I couldn't get to my desk and to my phone calls fast enough. I'm so grateful for the Spirit showing me what I needed to do and impressing upon me the urgency of obedience. Sure, it wasn't comfortable or easy, but it wasn't nearly as dreadful as I had feared. Restitution was made, and the peace and release and joy that it has brought has been amazing.

"My lifetime lesson: Do the hard and humbling work of restitution as soon as you can! Don't put it off or you might never do it, and it would be the only thing that is blocking you from receiving all God has for you."

"This week I e-mailed a former boss that I had harbored bitterness toward him and asked his forgiveness. I had always rationalized my anger toward him but couldn't escape the Holy Spirit's conviction about my part in the conflict. I had never felt that before—or maybe I just wasn't listening as closely as I am now. *What was the response?* It was O.K. The real victory was accomplished in me. I saw him the other day and, for the first time in years, thought nothing but the best of him. That's got to be the Lord's work in my heart! For the first time in a long time, I felt God's hand of blessing on my life. Flooding over me was a warmth that I once had known but had not felt for a long time."

What relationships in your past or present have been injured or broken because of your sin? Read again the link between restitution and repentance from pages 131–34. "Repentance is no longer concerned with the other person's part of the problem but confesses that *I* haven't been what *I'm* supposed to be so I'll make it right as much as I can and leave the rest with God. Repentance is doing what I need to do and what I can do."

Restitution Chart

Who do I need to write a letter of apology to? Who do I need to call and ask forgiveness? Who do I need to visit?

Names	Offenses	Action Needed?	When Can I Do This?
1.			
2.			
3.			
4.			
5.			

Complete the above restitution chart. Be very specific with yourself. In the context of the entire problem, your wrong may not even be the biggest piece—but it is your piece to make right.

You are repenting first before God (vertical), and then before the person whom your sin hurt (horizontal). This is unconditional repentance, not at all dependent on their response.

Restitution may mean more than an apology. Consider what your sin has cost them (money, reputation, etc.). Pay it back as far as you are able. Also write down when you are going to contact the person and how you are going to do so.

Ask a friend or mentor to give you prayer support as you follow through with this step. Report back to them the results of your restitution efforts. Trust me when I tell you this will be one of the greatest blessings you have ever experienced in your life.

Mark 4. Revival toward God

If you have done everything to this point exactly as I've written and if you've done it sincerely from your heart, there really isn't much for me to write here. You are already experiencing some raindrops of mercy.

Mark 5. Moving Forward

Repentance always takes you to a good place. It's never a waste of time. When you can break out of the self-condemning rut of the past and move forward into the freshness of a revived relationship with God, you'll know repentance is doing a work in your heart.

A big part of moving forward is going into the next chapter and allowing the grace of our Lord Jesus Christ to wash over the sin that you have handled His way! Turn the page. I can hear the thunder. Showers of joy are headed your way.

Far be it from me
to boast except in the cross
of our Lord Jesus Christ.

GALATIANS 6:14

CHAPTER 5

Christ on the Cross: A Picture of Grace

The cross of Jesus Christ is the signature symbol of the central event in the history of civilization. Not until the second century was the cross welcomed as the central symbol of Christianity. The emperor Constantine saw it in a vision and banned it as an instrument of execution. In fact, the cross was never thought of as anything but a hideous instrument of death until everyone who had actually seen a crucifixion had died off. Only then did people represent the cross as something sacred in sculpture, paintings, and other artistic forms.

Today, we depict the cross as common. Jewelers pound it into all sorts of finery so we can staple it to our ears and wear it around our necks. Merchandisers manufacture this symbol of unlimited atonement into fuzzy things for my rearview mirror or stand-ups for my garden. From teacups to T-shirts, the cross has cornered the market on crassness. Department stores hawk chocolate-covered ones for "holy week." Baseball players and businessmen cross themselves before a big moment. The cross itself has become big business. But it was never intended to be some lucky trinket. This is profanity in the truest sense. Is it any wonder we have lost the wonder of what happened on Calvary?

The resurrection of Christ was the event that accomplished salvation and verified Christ's victory over death. But it was the cross of Jesus Christ that showed us the grace of God. Everything that God wants us to know about Himself comes together in those crossbeams.

Our purpose in this chapter is to elevate the cross. Think on Him there. In your mind's eye, picture Jesus stretched out against the sky. What's He doing there? That's the question we will now explore. We'll focus our attention on the Gospel of Matthew to discover four answers to that question: What's Jesus doing on the cross?

What's Jesus Doing on the Cross? He's Substituting

Jesus lived His life on earth at a time of revolution and unrest in the nation of Israel. The Romans had conquered and subjugated the land, and every day Hebrew insurgents battled in the streets. People didn't need TV; they watched drama right in front of them as their hometown boys were captured as resistance fighters and injured, killed, or carted off to prison (definitely the underdogs compared to the forces of Rome). You can imagine how the families and communities suffered in the aftershock of such conflict on a daily basis.

So, with that background, we enter the story **at the time of the Passover.** This is Jewish culture's most celebrated time of year. They were commanded by the Old Testament to remember the exodus from Egypt (Exodus 12:43). Over the centuries it became like their Christmas and New Year's celebrations combined.

The "Passover party" culminated in the governor releasing a prisoner of the people's choice to appease their anger and reduce their frustration with the Roman occupation. Matthew 27:15 reports that at **the feast the governor was accustomed to release for the crowd any one prisoner whom they wanted.** This was Pilate's perfect opportunity to avert the murderous demands for Jesus' death by offering either Jesus or the most **noto-rious prisoner called Barabbas.** Pilate was trying to position Jesus as the favorite to be released. He said, "You choose. Do you want this mad revolutionary or Jesus?" He believed their sense of self-preservation would force them to choose

> *The resurrection of Christ was the event that accomplished salvation and verified Christ's victory over death. But it was the cross of Jesus Christ that showed us the grace of God.*

Jesus. Verse 17 says, **So when they had gathered, Pilate said to them, "Whom do you want me to release for you: Barabbas, or Jesus who is called Christ?"**

In effect, Pilate was offering, "Do you want Osama bin Laden or Jesus? The BTK murderer or Jesus?" Surely they would want Jesus. But Pilate **knew that it was out of envy that they had delivered him [Jesus] up.** While Pilate was sitting on the judgment seat, his wife sent word to him: **"Have nothing to do with that righteous man, for I have suffered much because of him today in a dream"** (vv. 18–19). Even Pilate's pagan wife was disturbed by the injustice being done to Christ. But the crowd was irrationally determined to see Christ die.

Now the chief priests and the elders persuaded the crowd to ask for Barabbas and destroy Jesus. *Destroy,* a very strong word, actually means "annihilate him," to erase not only His person, but the memory of His having ever lived. Wipe Him out so He never existed. Verse 21 records the question again: **The governor again said to them, "Which of the two do you want me to release**

for you?" And they said, "Barabbas." Pilate said to them, "Then what shall I do with Jesus who is called Christ?" They all said, "Let him be crucified!" Pilate was stunned, knowing that Barrabas was dangerous and Jesus was innocent. So he asked, "Why, what evil has he done?"

Everyone knew the evil that Barabbas had done. Jesus was crucified between **two robbers.** Other translations say, "thieves." In the original language, "robbers" doesn't refer to burglar types who comb neighborhoods looking for homes where the owners forgot to lock their patio doors. It literally means "revolutionaries." The two men crucified on either side of Jesus were revolutionaries. It was the cross intended for Barabbas, the most notorious revolutionary, in between the other two revolutionaries upon which Jesus died. For that reason, it is not stretching it at all to say that Jesus literally, physically took the cross that had been reserved for Barabbas. Jesus died in Barabbas's place.

You can't understand the gospel until you understand this idea of substitution. Jesus died first for Barabbas and then for every other member of the human race who has ever lived. Barabbas is the first in the line, but behind him stands someone else and so on and so on. I am there in that line. You are too. Each of us deserves to die in payment for our own sin, but Jesus stepped in and took that penalty for us. I deserve to die that death, but the gift of God is eternal life *through Jesus Christ*. That's substitution. Jesus took *my* place on the cross. This is the central tenet of the historic gospel; without this there is nothing else to say.

Picture Christ on the cross and ask yourself: "What's He doing there?" Answer: He's subbing for you. He's taking God's wrath for your sin. He's satisfying the just demands of a holy God. He's paying the price that God's holiness requires so you and I can be forgiven.

Romans 6:23 says, **The wages of sin is death, but the free gift of God is eternal life through Jesus Christ our Lord.** Second Corinthians 5:21 says, **For our sake he made him to be sin who knew no sin, so that in him we might become the righteousness of God.**

What's Jesus doing on the cross? He's substituting: Jesus in my place. My heart overflows with gratitude when I think of Jesus Christ taking upon Himself the penalty that was mine to bear! God demonstrated such love that **while we were still sinners, Christ died for us** (Romans 5:8).

What's Jesus Doing on the Cross? He's Scandalizing

The cross is an outrageous offense. It doesn't matter from what vantage point you stand or where you grew up or what you know. The cross makes scandalous claims that cause intense reactions.

Pilate was so smug and self-assured that even the over-the-top bloodthirsty crowd unsettled him. **So when Pilate saw that he was gaining nothing, but rather that a riot was beginning, he took water and washed his hands before the crowd, saying, "I am innocent of this man's blood; see to it yourselves"** (Matthew 27:24).

The Jews, rejecting Christ, called out for His crucifixion. Crucifixion was the most shameful, painful, awful death that a person could experience, and they wanted it for Jesus. They passionately pleaded for Christ's torturous death in a way that defies explanation. Review just the highlights of the scandalous treatment of Jesus Christ found in Matthew 27:27–44:

> **Then the soldiers of the governor took Jesus into the governor's headquarters, and they gathered the whole battalion [600 soldiers] before him. And they**

**stripped him and put a scarlet robe on him, and twist-
ing together a crown of thorns, they put it on his head
and put a reed in his right hand. And kneeling before
him, they mocked him** [meaning they made him look
like a fool], . . . **And they spit on him . . . . And when
they had mocked him, they stripped him of the robe
. . . and led him away to crucify him. . . . They offered
him wine to drink, mixed with gall** [a narcotic to dull
the pain], **but when he tasted it, he would not drink it.
. . . Those who passed by derided him, wagging their
heads and saying, . . . "He saved others; he cannot save
himself." . . . And the robbers who were crucified with
him also reviled him in the same way.**

First the Romans, then the Jewish leaders, now even the crimi-
nals take their shot at the Savior on the cross. What a scandal! The
dictionary defines a scandal as that which causes a public outcry
and produces an expression of malicious sentiment. The cross of
Jesus Christ has always been irrationally and inexplicably an outrageous scandal.

Why the irrational hatred of Jesus Christ? Why the illogical
animosity toward our Lord? Without explanation, it goes on to
this day everywhere around us. If you doubt this reality, take some
pagan friend out for dinner this weekend. Everything will be wonderful at dinner as you converse on a variety of subjects until you
bring up your love for Jesus Christ and the forgiveness found only
in the gospel. Then get ready.

You can follow Mohammed or Ghandi or any religion of the
East; you can be a washed-out liberal Christian or a closet Cath-
olic and everything will be wonderful. You can be for abortion,
pro-homosexual, and support every liberal agenda in the country,

and polite company will, at worst, smile with deference. In fact, you can be passionate about absolutely anything and you will be applauded for your commitment. Not until someone whose heart is in the grip of this world finds out that you have given your heart to Jesus Christ and that He is the greatest treasure of your heart will you begin to experience intense hatred and irrational behavior.

Irrational Hatred of Christ and His Cross Goes to Washington

I was invited recently along with thirty other pastors to a White House briefing. What a privilege! In the past the President has met with us personally in an off-the-record meeting, but on this occasion he sent a top White House official to brief us on the spiritual battle raging in our country in the highest political arenas.

On the day we were there, the President announced his new Supreme Court nominee, Harriet Miers. We were told of her testimony as a devoted, born-again follower of Jesus Christ. She came to Christ in the early 1980s, and she loves the Lord. As I heard firsthand about what my heart had hoped for, I knew that her nomination would never stand. Within days the press poured out a vitriolic, irrational hatred of her that seemed to shock even the abuse-hardened Washington insiders. No sooner had Ms. Miers acknowledged her adult conversion and her ongoing love of the Savior than those who represent the kingdom of darkness began a scandalous assault upon her life and record until withdrawal of her nomination was her only choice. Even some of the so-called Christ-less conservatives opposed her in a way that defied all logic and reason.

What happens in Washington also happens in your city and on your street. The very forces of darkness are leveling their greatest attacks against those who would lift high the cross of Jesus Christ.

Irrationality on My Street

There used to be a little boy in our neighborhood who would come over to our house. He had the bad habit of taking the Lord's name in vain. His parents were not concerned that he did so and did not correct him. As a habit, I do not correct other people's children—unless they're on my front porch. One day I heard him calling out the name of Christ repeatedly in a blasphemous tone, so I told him gently and by name, "We love Jesus Christ here at our house, and you can't speak of Him in such a disrespectful way when you are at our home. He's everything to us. He loves you, and you shouldn't talk about Him like that." I thought that was the end of it until his parents found out that I had corrected him. I met with them and tried to calmly request that our beliefs be respected on our property.

Well, our relationship with these otherwise fine people never recovered, and they have had an irrational anger and hatred toward us from that day forward. Even recently, my daughter saw the same boy on a school bus (now, five years later). Had he forgotten the issue? I don't think so, or he wouldn't have gotten right in her face screaming the name of Jesus Christ. Would that have happened if we were Hindu or Hare Krishna? It's so irrational; how do you explain it?

It's All about the Cross

There's a battle going on as Satan and his demonic army spend themselves to incite hatred against the cross of Jesus Christ. Very few are neutral in this battle; most are firmly entrenched and fighting on one side or the other. When you live for Christ and express to others the message of the cross, you're going to experience this scandalizing hatred.

What's Jesus doing on that cross? He's fighting for the souls of men. He's seeking to redeem them from their own scandalizing hatred. Hear the soldiers laughing and mocking as the Savior gives up His life for them. Two thousand years later, people still scream and mock the cross of Jesus. It's a scandal!

What's Jesus Doing on the Cross? He's Suffering

When they had crucified him (v. 35). Who can come close to detailing all that this phrase means? Isaiah 52:14 tells us that Jesus' **appearance was so marred** that he didn't look like a man. These historical realities are more firmly fixed in our mind's eye since Mel Gibson's movie *The Passion of the Christ,* which is actually a toned-down version of Christ's suffering. As brutal as it was to watch, it doesn't come close to capturing the excruciating suffering of Jesus on the cross. Did you know the word *excruciating* actually comes from the Latin term meaning "out of the cross"?

In his book, *The Life of Christ,* Frederick Farrar said: "A death by crucifixion seems to include all that pain and death have to offer . . . horrible and ghastly. Dizziness, cramps, thirst, starvation, sleeplessness, traumatic fever, shame, publicity of shame, long continuance of torment, horror of anticipation, mortification of intended wounds. All intensified just up unto the point they can be endured at all. All stopping just short of the point that would give the sufferer relief of unconsciousness."

One thing is clear: first-century executions were not like modern ones. They did not seek a quick, painless death or the preservation of any measure of dignity. On the contrary, they sought an agonizing torture that completely humiliated the victim. To fully appreciate the meaning of the cross of Christ you have to comprehend the extent to which He *suffered* for our sin.

As much as it is often our focus, the physical pain was the lesser issue in Jesus' suffering. Notice this in Matthew 27:45–50: **Now from the sixth hour there was darkness** [a symbol of God turning away] **over all the land until the ninth hour. And about the ninth hour Jesus cried out with a loud voice, saying, "Eli, Eli, lema sabachthani?" that is, "My God, my God, why have you forsaken me?"**

> *All God's righteous hatred of all that sin from all of human history was poured out upon Christ as He hung there on that cross.*

In those words we hear the deeper suffering of the cross. Scholars debate the number of statements Jesus made from Golgotha, but this much is clear: only one referred even slightly to His physical suffering. He said simply, **"I thirst"** (John 19:28). What Christ said beyond that reveals to us that His greater suffering by far was the separation from His Father.

Through endless, countless eons of time that stretch from the base of infinity, Jesus had known only perfect unity with His Father. Now as He hung on the cross, He experienced total separation from that perfect unity. What finite mind can comprehend separating the inseparable? Forsaken by the Father? A love that was infinitely deep, eternal, and everlasting was lost in that darkness.

Now it would be one thing if Jesus was simply separated from the dark-hearted, pagan people screaming insults at Him and headed for hell themselves. Abandonment by pagans meant nothing. It's still another thing for Jesus to be abandoned by the weak-willed disciples who were following at a distance anyway. Certainly there was pain in that, but He had a realistic understanding of their weakness. But to have done nothing wrong and to be abandoned by God the Father. Nothing compares to that kind of suffering. That is the suffering of the cross.

The more I study the Gospels, the more I recognize that all points come to a screeching halt right here. The Gospels race through the life of Christ. Three chapters cover the thirty years of His birth and growth to manhood. Twenty-two chapters cover the three years of ministry. But then incredibly, a single week takes three lengthy chapters and two of those are devoted to three hours around the cross. It's as if everything goes into slow motion. Everything slows to a grueling pace as the Scriptures halt their progression to highlight just this: the cross of Jesus Christ.

What's Jesus Doing on the Cross? He's Satisfying

If the cross of Jesus Christ is the central target that all biblical content is shooting at, the subject of how His death satisfies the wrath of God is the bull's-eye. The gospel of Jesus Christ is only a concept until we comprehend the way in which Jesus' death on the cross satisfied God's wrath for sin.

Matthew 27:51 reports, **And behold, the curtain of the temple was torn in two, from top to bottom. And the earth shook, and the rocks were split.** The temple represented God's presence, and the Holy of Holies was the place where God dwelt in the back of the temple, behind an impenetrable curtain. The curtain was at least eight inches thick. No one went behind that curtain. This is where God dwelt in unapproachable holiness. Only the priest was allowed to go into the Holy of Holies and then only once a year. The curtain reminded everyone of the sin that separated man and God.

How awesome then to read in Matthew 27:50–51 that at the precise moment Jesus **cried out again with a loud voice and yielded up his spirit** that immediately **the curtain of the temple was torn in two, *from top to bottom*** (emphasis added). The temple curtain was what kept people out of God's presence, but at that moment Jesus died as an atoning sacrifice for sin. He suffered and was substituted and has satisfied the wrath of a holy God against sin, and the way is open to God. In the instant Jesus died, the veil in the temple was torn in two. Not from bottom to top as if a man was standing there saying we don't need this anymore, but from top to bottom because God Himself reached down and tore the symbol of His separation from each of us. Sin is now paid for. "The way is open," He declares. "Come into My presence. Wrath is averted. My Son has paid the price for your sin. Evil, sinful men can now approach holiness." Why? Because of the cross. God says with this action of tearing the temple veil: "Sin has been paid for. Satisfied!"

In fact, God wanted us to know that something had changed for all time. Not only was the curtain torn, but God Himself reached down and shook the earth and said, "I want people to know something is happening—pay attention!" Look at this: **The tombs also were opened. And many bodies of the saints who had fallen asleep were raised** [it's like the original thriller!], **and coming out of the tombs after his resurrection they went into the holy city and appeared to many** (vv. 52–53). The natural order of birth and death was reversed. Again, a sign from heaven said, "Pay attention. Something big is happening here." It's unparalleled. It's unprecedented. Nothing like this will ever happen again.

God is satisfied in the cross of Jesus Christ. So awesome and obviously supernatural was all of this that the Scripture records: **When the centurion and those who were with him, keeping watch over Jesus, saw the earthquake and what took place, they were filled with awe and said, "Truly this was the Son of God!"** (v. 54).

I wonder if we can imagine just how much God hates sin. God hates sin with an infinite loathing that we can't comprehend.

Think of every act of cruel barbarism that twists your stomach into a knot. Think of every act of perversity measured out against pure innocence by rampant, heartless perversion. Think of the sickening things happening in this moment that no one will ever know about except God. Also in this moment, at this very second, the totality of that wickedness rises like it always has and will, as an unceasing stench to the nostrils of God.

> When Jesus said,
> "It is finished,"
> God said,
> "Paid in full."

Some people ask, "Why doesn't God do something about sin?" Newsflash: He did. All God's righteous hatred of all that sin from all of human history was poured out upon Christ as He hung there on that cross. On Him almighty judgment fell that would have sunk the world to hell.

A holy God poured out His wrath on His innocent Son so that we could be forgiven. When Jesus said, "It is finished," God said, "Paid in full." Sin has been put away now. In a way we will never fully comprehend, the cross of Jesus Christ satisfied the requirements of a holy God.

Paul declared, **Far be it from me to boast except in the cross of our Lord Jesus Christ** (Galatians 6:14).

Four Pictures of Grace

Because God gave Jesus the penalty for our sin while He hung on that cross, God can give us something else, something that we don't deserve—grace. Everything we have ever received from God is because of grace. God doesn't give paychecks; God gives grace. Unearned, undeserved, unmerited—that's grace. To understand and embrace the impact of grace in your life, I want us to review passages of Scripture that teach us what grace is and what grace does.

From the Life of Peter:
A Picture of God's Grace
Luke 22:54–62; John 21

To Peter, that moment by the fire in Caiaphas's courtyard marked the greatest crisis of his life. He must have relived the scene over and over again, wishing to snatch back his words, "I do not know Him!" He had spit out that denial not once, but three times. Somewhere in the night, a rooster stretched its neck and punctuated his faith's failure. In that horrid moment, Peter looked over his shoulder and caught the eye of the One who loved him more than life, passing through the courtyard on His way to the cross. That moment between sinner and Savior must have hung in the air like a framed picture.

Peter turned his face from the fire and wept. What burned more? The fire's acrid smoke that blew into his eyes or the conviction of the sin that pierced his heart?

Wasn't it earlier that same night that Peter had vowed, "Others will turn away, Lord, but I won't"?

Go ahead and be hard on Peter. Talk about how impulsive he was or how he shot off his mouth. He probably had heard the rebuke all the time. But something happened that changed Peter between that devastating moment by this fire and when he stood with the Lord by another fire a couple of mornings later.

In those days in-between, Peter's guilt could have driven him to the cynical edge: *What was I thinking to believe He was the Christ, anyway?* He could have run, never to return. His heart could have become hardened with unbelief. For sure, if you don't deal with your sin, it can drive you to some awful places.

But that's not the Peter we meet three days later rushing into Jesus' empty tomb (John 20:3–9), or the Peter who throws himself into the lake to get to Jesus (John 21:7–9), or the Peter Jesus pulls aside in private conversation and restores to friendship and ministry (John 21:15–17). Did they speak of that awful moment by the fire? We don't know; that's between them. What we do know is that Peter's crisis had taken him to the right place with God. Sin, rightly understood, prompted repentance. And repentance had turned him around to meet the face of grace.

This then is revival. Peter recognized his sin. He rightly understood his problem. He turned away from his sin and to the Lord, and then the grace made possible by Jesus Christ's ransom on the cross released him from sin's power. Peter returned to the Lord with a whole heart—stronger, more humble, ready for greater days ahead. That's revival.

Grace that Redeems—the Penalty Is Gone

He [the Father] has delivered us from the domain of darkness and transferred us to the kingdom of his beloved Son, in whom we have redemption, the forgiveness of sins (Colossians 1:13–14).

Apart from Christ, we belong to the kingdom of darkness, but because of grace, our penalty is gone.

Where would you be today apart from God's grace? You would be in the kingdom of darkness. If you have the privilege of knowing Jesus Christ personally through faith in Him, how exactly did you get that relationship? Did God look down and say, "You're kind of better than average. I think I'll take you." Is that how it happened? No. There was nothing special about you or me or anyone who has received His grace. God wasn't drawn to us in any way. He extended His unearned, undeserved, unmerited grace to us.

God *chose* to set His love upon you. He reached down and took hold of you—and looking back you realize that you couldn't have even resisted Him. He came after you. He conquered your will. He drew you to Himself. He loves You. That's grace.

Apart from Christ, our citizenship is in hell. There is no way out. The storm of His wrath was coming upon you like the urban poor of New Orleans just before Hurricane Katrina. We were trapped with no way out, and the waters of God's wrath were rising until Christ stepped in and led our souls to higher ground. Without that grace, we would have drowned.

Verse 14 says, **We have redemption, the forgiveness of sin.** That pictures Christ's death as payment to God. He didn't just come and get us; He paid a price to get us back. Do you know what it means to be forgiven of your sin? It means that no wrong that you've ever done can be held against you. Think of all the sin lingering in your imperfect memory of the past. In Christ, it cannot be held against you. It's unbelievable! In Him, we have redemption through

His blood. We have the forgiveness of sins. Can you even take it in? We have been spared the horror of God's wrath in hell. As Satan and his demonic host are heading for an eternal home in the lake of fire, they will notice that a few of us are gone . . . because of God's grace.

Apart from Christ, we are bankrupt with nothing to offer in payment. Have you ever been totally bankrupt?

> *As Satan and his demonic host are heading for an eternal home in the lake of fire, they will notice that a few of us are gone . . . because of God's grace.*

When I was a college student, I had nothing—not two cents. I couldn't even afford to live in the dorm. One night very late, I was driving home in an old, broken-down car when I got stopped by the police because my tail light was out. He pulled me over, took my license, then returned to say, "Do you know you have several unpaid parking tickets?"

"Uh . . . I think that's probably right."

"Since they're long overdue, our policy is that you have to pay them right now." I took out my wallet, and can you believe I didn't have a single cent? "Then you're going to have to pay by credit card."

"I don't have a credit card."

"Then you'll have to come with me."

So I got in the back of his squad car and headed back to town. Somehow on the way I convinced the officer to drop by the dormitory of my college. There in the middle of the night, I woke a few friends with the police officer's light shining over my shoulder and scrounged up enough money to barely pay my fines.

Without intervention from another source I was headed to jail. I could not pay the debt myself. Sincerity could not pay my debt. Good efforts or better behavior could not pay my debts. My only hope of avoiding jail time was the willing payment of others. Without that help I was 100 percent bankrupt.

That is the condition of every single person in this world—bankrupt with no capacity to pay, nothing with which to appease the wrath of a holy God. What in your life could satisfy God's demand for perfection? Nothing—only God can. When we are bankrupt, not able to satisfy God's demands, God Himself steps in and pays the price for us. It's outrageous! As the hymn proclaims, "Marvelous grace of our loving God, freely bestowed on all who believe . . . Grace that is greater than all my sin." No wonder we call it amazing.

Grace that Releases—the Power Is Gone

For sin will have no dominion over you, since you are not under law but under grace (Romans 6:14).

But that's not all! If you only know the grace that redeems and not the grace that releases, you're like an astronaut, all strapped in the space shuttle but still on the launch pad. If you only know the grace that redeems and not the grace that releases, you're like a mountain climber at base camp.

The best stuff is up ahead! So many of Jesus' followers settle for just the fire insurance. They experience the forgiveness from the *penalty* of sin but not release from the *power* of sin in their life going forward. I've got phenomenal news: there's more to this grace than simply a home in heaven. There's a grace that releases you from the power of sin here and now. Do you want more of that?

Romans 6:14 says, **For sin will have no dominion over you, since you are not under law but under grace.** All the law can do is make you feel like a failure. But you're not under the law anymore; sin doesn't have to have dominion over you. The word *dominion* is both official and functional authority—as in, not just the police at your door, but the police at your door with a gun to your head and your hands behind your back. That's the way sin had dominion over me before I came to Christ. Sin would say, "Jump," and I would say, "How high?" Now sin says, "Jump," and I say, "Get lost! You're not in charge anymore. I don't have to do what you say. I'm under grace now. My life belongs to Christ, and I want to do what He wants me to do." You have the freedom to choose what is right. You can please God. You can live a life of righteousness. Grace makes personal, experiential righteousness possible.

> *Grace is the oxygen of Christian living once we have dealt with sin God's way through personal repentance.*

You say, "Righteousness is the last word that I would use to describe my experience this past week." Hey, get up! God loves you. Christ declares you righteous because of your personal faith in Him. You can begin again. The power of sin is broken—the choice is yours. Embrace that truth and live in it.

Experience the grace that releases. John 8:36 says, **"If the Son sets you free, you will be free indeed."** That's the power of the gospel. If you only have grace that redeems, and not the grace that releases, you're just at base camp, man. There's so much more for you up ahead. Let God give it to you.

You're under grace. It doesn't matter what Satan says to you, it doesn't matter what your past says about you, it doesn't matter what people who don't love you say about you. Here's what God says about you: you're under His grace. Grace is what He sees; grace is what He knows. Grace is the oxygen of Christian living once we have dealt with sin God's way through personal repentance.

Grace that Reconciles—the Prejudice Is Gone

**For he [Jesus] himself is our peace,
who has made us both one (Ephesians 2:14).**

Ours isn't the first century when there's been racial and social unrest. In Paul's day, a fierce tension raged between Jews and Gentiles, even within the walls of the early church. Paul writes in Ephesians 2:14 that Jesus **has broken down in his flesh the dividing wall of hostility.** By allowing Himself to be crucified as a substitute for our sin, Jesus broke down the barriers that separate us from one another. That's not only a better relationship with God, but a new heart for others, especially those who, humanly speaking, would be harder for you to love. God's grace causes us to seek reconciliation with people in every race, class, and culture. That's why the church of Jesus Christ should be the most diverse place in all of society. Christ has broken down the walls that separate us. Grace reconciles us—it makes us one. People who don't normally get together do so at the cross of Jesus Christ.

I live in Chicago, and "hostility" best describes the relationship between people all around us. Too often the focus is on what divides us—different races, different social classes, different backgrounds. "You're not like me," we say. "I don't know you." God forgive us. God intends grace to sweep all of that darkness out of our hearts. **That he might create in himself one new man in place of the two, so making peace, and might reconcile us both to God in one body through the cross, thereby killing the hostility** (Ephesians 2:15–16). Do you know what that means? Not just right with God, but right with others.

When you come to know Jesus Christ by faith and experience God's grace, you get a love for people like you've never known. You encounter people different from you, and you find yourself trying to bridge that separation. That's grace alive in you. You meet people who are educationally different from you and you love them. You observe people who are culturally different from you and you love them. You get with people who are racially different from you and you love them.

It takes a lot of courage and faith to come to a church where you are not the majority. In our church I frequently embrace and publicly thank the so-called "minorities" (we are all minorities somewhere in the world) that are choosing to worship with us. They are enriching the worship and the glory that goes to Jesus Christ because what they're really saying is, "I belong with people who belong with Jesus even though they're different from me in many other ways." That kind of effort takes courage and reflects grace. Together we are saying, "Even if we look different, even if our backgrounds are different, whatever is different, this is the same—we love and follow Jesus Christ." That's what the cross of Jesus does—it reconciles people.

> The church of Jesus Christ should be the most diverse place in all of society. Christ has broken down the walls . . . . Grace reconciles us— it makes us one.

If you've experienced God's grace, you ought to hate prejudice. I never really knew racial prejudice while growing up, but my first semester in college was spent at a school in Tennessee. I'll never forget sitting in the dorm room with a bunch of guys, playing a game and eating popcorn when an African-American brother walked into the room. I said, "Hey dude, how's it going?" and offered him some popcorn. He took some in his hands, hung out for a few minutes, and then quietly left. Only when he was gone did I realize that the other guys would not eat from that bowl again. That realization sickened me. I left that school after only one semester. Now, I'm not attributing that wicked attitude to the

South, the North, the East, or the West; I'm just telling you that what happened was wrong. It was deeply evil. I had never seen it before, and I will never forget it.

Every follower of Jesus Christ—whatever your race, denomination, or social background—ought to hate prejudice of every kind with a holy indignation. If you've experienced the grace of the cross of Christ, there ought to be something in you that repudiates this unfounded, over-generalized, stereotyped thinking formed without a solid assessment of the facts. All are one in Christ. That's the power of grace—it reconciles.

Grace that Removes—My Past Is Gone
You, who were dead in your trespasses . . . God made alive together with him, having forgiven us all our trespasses, by canceling the record of debt that stood against us (Colossians 2:13–14).

You might say, "My issue is not how I see those who are different than me. My issue is how I see myself. My problem is the choices I have made, the things I have done. When I think of living in God's grace, the biggest barrier is what I see in me." Do you realize that the entire body of Christ is made up of people like you? We have all experienced grace because we have all come to understand that we really needed it.

Notice this: **And you, who were dead in your trespasses . . . God made alive together with him, having forgiven us all our trespasses, by canceling the record of debt that stood against us with its legal demands. This he set aside, nailing it to the cross** (Colossians 2:13–14). Grace outrageously asserts that all past sins are wiped away because of the cross.

- How can a murderous revolutionary dying for his actions receive the promise of eternal "paradise" just because he comes around at the last minute (Luke 23:42)? It's called grace.

- Why would a man stoop to help his sworn enemy who had been robbed and beaten (the religious dudes all took a pass) and then spend himself to see his health and strength restored (Luke 10:33–35)? It's called grace.
- How can a guy who shows up for the last part of the day after others had been slaving for hours in the hot sun get the exact same pay (Matthew 20:8–15)? It's called grace.
- Why does the son who lived like a pig and then moved in with the pigs get to be forgiven, restored, and have a party thrown in his honor (Luke 15:11–31)? It's called grace.

A listing of amazing grace stories in the New Testament could fill many pages. Each one is shocking, outrageous, unearned, and undeserved. It's called grace!

Where Is My Past Now?

Believe me when I tell you that God does not want His children wallowing in a past that He has forgiven. If you're wondering what happened to all the wrong you so deeply regret, hear it now again: **By canceling the record of debt that stood against us with its legal demands. This he set aside, nailing it to the cross** (Colossians 2:14).

Sometimes the greatest barrier is the way we see ourselves. We won't live in the grace that God proclaims over us. We won't embrace and experience the immense freedom that true grace gives. I read again this week the story of Maryann Bird, who wrote the following in her book *The Whisper Test*.

> I grew up knowing I was different. I hated it. I was born with a cleft palate and when I started school, my classmates made it clear to me how I looked to others. A

Worshipping the Wounded Savior—
Zinzendorf and the Moravian Revival (1727)

Nicholas von Zinzendorf, a nobleman by birth, had been single-focused since childhood. His life motto was, "I have one passion: it is Jesus, Jesus only."*

Yet in spite of his long-time commitment to Christ, he was unprepared to be so moved by God's Spirit while visiting an art gallery in Duesseldorf. His attention was captured by a painting of Christ on the cross, "Ecce Homo," over which were the words: "This have I done for thee; what doest thou for Me?"* Stirred by this challenge, Zinzendorf returned to his estate. For several years, he had provided shelter to a couple of hundred religious refugees from Moravia, and it was to these brothers that he brought home this stirring message from the suffering Savior.

On August 13, 1727, this group of committed men celebrated the Lord's Supper. As they focused their worship on the wounded Savior, their hearts were filled with love for Him who had died for them. They sensed an awesome presence of the living Christ. That event forever changed Zinzendorf and the rest of that assembly.

Look at the difference the Savior made in their lives from that day forward:

- On August 24, forty-eight men and women began the practice that two people each hour around the clock would pray for Christ's kingdom work around the world. This began what became known as the "Hundred Year Prayer Meeting" as others took up the task of praying for missions.
- Over one hundred of those present at that initial Lord's Supper eventually went around the world to "win for the Lamb that was slain the rewards of His suffering." Most worked to earn a living so they could preach the gospel free of charge.
- The first two missionaries sent out from the group went to St. Thomas in the West Indies. They had been told that the slave owners would not permit them to preach to the slaves, so they left Germany intent on selling themselves into slavery so they would be able to share the gospel freely. Upon arriving in St. Thomas they found an open door.
- Another group of Moravian missionaries met John Wesley on a boat headed for America. He was so impacted by their living faith in Christ that he began to evaluate his own faith. Later in 1738 at a Moravian chapel begun by another group of missionaries, John Wesley was converted. He went to Germany to meet Zinzendorf and these Moravians who had so deeply loved Christ. Wesley went on from there to lead the Evangelical Revival in England and the First Great Awakening in America.

God had used a quiet moment in an art gallery and a picture of grace to spark a wildfire of revived hearts that spread to thousands in England and the American colonies.

*John Greenfield, *Power from On High: The Story of the Great Moravian Revival of 1727* (Bethlehem, Pa.: The Moravian Church in America, 1928), 20.

little girl, with a misshapen lip, a crooked nose, lopsided teeth, and garbled speech. When schoolmates asked, "What happened to your lip?" I'd tell them I'd fallen and cut it on a piece of glass. Somehow it seemed more acceptable to have suffered an accident rather than to have been born different. I was convinced that no one else other than my family could love me.

There was, however, a teacher in the second grade we all adored. Mrs. Leonard, by name. She was short, round, happy. A sparkling lady. Annually, we had a hearing test. Mrs. Leonard gave it to everyone in the class. And finally it was my turn. I knew from past years as we stood against the door and covered one ear, the teacher, sitting at her desk, would whisper something and we would have to say back what we heard her say. "The sky is blue." Or "Do you have new shoes?" I waited for her words—the words that God must have put in her mouth—the seven words that changed my life. Mrs. Leonard whispered, "I wish you were my little girl."*

> *God says to every person deformed by sin, "I wish you were Mine. I wish you were Mine."*

God says to every person deformed by sin, "I wish you were Mine. I wish you were Mine." This is the power of the grace of God. Will you let it be yours?

Maybe you don't feel worthy of God's love. Maybe you're ashamed of where you've been and what you've done. You wonder if you could ever feel clean again. Sin is not a trifle; but if you've been reading carefully and doing the exercises in these pages, you

*www.net153.com/magazine/subscription/inspirationalstories/the_whisper.htm

know that very well by now. Holiness is God's standard, and when we really comprehend what that means we are overwhelmed by the sin we see in the mirror. Real repentance from that sin brings us finally and in exhaustion to the place where grace has been waiting all along. Not until we fully grasp the gravity of our sin problem can we grasp the amazing solution that God has provided by grace. Christ on the cross is the 3-D, Technicolor, IMAX, to the max, living picture of God's grace: grace to redeem us from the penalty of sin, release us from the power of sin, reconcile us to one another, and remove the shame of our past.

ACTIVATE

Worship God in Spirit and Truth

We have pondered together the great grace of God in sending Jesus to die in our place. The next best thing we can do now is worship Him. Many great hymns and worship songs find their basis in Scripture. If you know this song, "How Deep the Father's Love for Us," sing it aloud to the Lord. If you don't know its tune, read it aloud. Next, look up and read the Scripture verses listed at the end of each line. Worship God in spirit and in truth with what you discover about His Son's death, life, and resurrection.

How Deep the Father's Love for Us

How deep the Father's love for us, how vast beyond all measure
(Romans 5:8)
That He should give His only Son to make a wretch His treasure.
(John 3:16–17)
How great the pain of searing loss, the Father turned His face away
(Mark 15:34)
As wounds which mar the chosen One, bring many sons to glory.
(Hebrews 2:10)

Behold the Man upon a cross, my sin upon His shoulders
      (John 19:5)
Ashamed, I hear my mocking voice call out among the scoffers.
      (Matthew 27:40)
It was my sin that held Him there until it was accomplished
      (Acts 4:10)
His dying breath has brought me life; I know that it is finished.
      (John 19:30)

I will not boast in anything: no gifts, no power, no wisdom
      (2 Corinthians 12:5)
But I will boast in Jesus Christ; His death and resurrection.
      (Galatians 6:14)
Why should I gain from His reward? I cannot give an answer
      (Philippians 3:8)
But this I know with all my heart: His wounds have paid my ransom. *
      (Matthew 20:28)

Nail It to the Cross

1. Get out your list of the sins that God is showing you.

2. Answer the following questions (there's a really good pay-off if you do!):

- Do you see this sin for what it is?
  Do you feel the weight of it?
  ❏Yes, I'm certain   ❏I'm beginning to   ❏No ❏No reply

- Have you confessed it to the Lord
  and asked for forgiveness?
  ❏Yes, I'm certain   ❏I think so   ❏No ❏No reply

- Have you repented of it and made any
  necessary restitution?
  ❏Yes, I'm certain   ❏I think so   ❏Not yet   ❏No reply

*Stuart Townsend; ©1995 Kingsway Thank You Music, CCLI #1596342; on the album *I Could Sing of Your Love Forever 2*.

3. Now read Colossians 2:13–14 again with this process in mind: **And you, who were dead in your trespasses . . . God made alive together with him, having forgiven us all our trespasses, by canceling the record of debt that stood against us with its legal demands. This he set aside, nailing it to the cross.**

God now wants to take that sin that you've repented of by His grace and nail it to the cross of Christ. It's not your problem any more. Colossians 2:14 is very clear—the debt is cancelled; the sin is nailed to the cross.

What tangible symbol could help you remember this fact that your sin is now surrendered to God? The next time you are tempted to choose that sin again or if Satan whispers that God's forgiveness couldn't cover it, remind yourself that the blood of Christ cleanses you from that sin and you now have the power over it. You're dead to it and alive to Christ. Share your symbol of forgiven sin with someone who prays for you and rejoice together with this new reminder.

> *Testimony about grace:* "From the way that I was raised, I had no problem seeing my sin being nailed to the cross. I just never saw that anything could be done about it. Every week I would go back to church and there it was, still pinned there. Since coming to Christ for salvation through grace by faith alone, I have struggled with my sin being forgiven once and for all. Every time Pastor James led us in the prayer of salvation, I would ask God for salvation all over again, just in case. Now I see I don't have to do that any more. My sin is not my problem after I confess it and forsake it and give it to Christ; it's His problem, and He takes care of it. He's forgiven my lifetime of rebellion, and He forgives me daily when I get that sin to the cross.

And the fact that He isn't on that cross any more is proof
that God has accepted Christ's sacrifice. Wow! What a
break-through for me."

ELEVATE

*Lord, thank You for the picture of Your grace in the cross of
Your dear Son. How great is Your love for Your children—and that
includes me. How unceasing. How unending. How unparalleled.
How unprecedented. Where could I ever find such grace that my
heart so desperately needs?*

*Lord, thank You that my failures of the past are nailed to the cross.
You have canceled the debt that is against me from everything about
which I feel secretly ashamed. The enemy would say that my best days
are behind me. But You say that there is yet an opportunity for me to
be the man or woman of righteousness that I am now becoming in You.
There's still time. Today is a new beginning for me. Today I start in
grace. How could I continue in sin now that I know what it cost You?
Thank You for Your presence here and now. I draw near to You. In Jesus'
name. Amen.*

REPLICATE

The great thing about grace is that it's meant to be shared. By
definition, it is demonstrable. In this chapter we explored four pictures of grace.

1. Grace that Redeems—the Penalty Is Gone (Colossians 2:13–14)

Ask yourself: Where would I be today apart from God's grace?
What future would I have to look forward to in this life and in eternity? Tell someone about how far you've come—by grace. Compare what life was like for you B.C. (Before Christ) with what it is
like today. Share Colossians 2:13–14 with them.

2. Grace that Releases—the Power Is Gone (Romans 6:13–14)

Ask yourself: How have my choices changed under grace? Do I choose to live under sin's control, or am I experiencing the power of God to say "No"? Am I living as free as I am? Tell someone about how your choices have changed since you've come to Christ, or even as recently as you've begun this study. Describe for them what used to be your preference and by the grace of God, how that desire has changed.

3. Grace that Reconciles—the Prejudice Is Gone (Ephesians 2:14)

Ask yourself: Who have I stiff-armed, either in attitude or action? Do I need to ask God's forgiveness for my arrogance in thinking I'm better than they are? Am I willing for God to bring someone different from me up close and personal? Do I hate prejudice as much as I should? Be a model of God's grace to someone who used to be to you behind a barrier of prejudice. Create an opportunity to get to know them. Ask them how you can pray for them—and then pray for them and even with them.

4. Grace that Removes—the Past Is Gone (Colossians 2:13–14)

Ask yourself: Is there anything from my past that I am still dragging around with me? Have I asked God to forgive me for it? Have I repented of it? Then what is my problem?—Give it up to God and get on with life. Someone you know thinks that God could never forgive them of things in their past. Ask God for the discernment and the words in leading them to the grace of God, whether they have yet to receive Christ's offer of salvation or if they are a struggling Christian. Assure them that we have all experienced grace because we have all come to understand that we really need it. The ground is level at the cross—and the future is bright!

I have been crucified with Christ.

It is no longer I who live,

but Christ who lives in me.

GALATIANS 2:20

And do not get drunk with wine,

for that is debauchery,

but be filled with the Spirit.

EPHESIANS 5:18

You, however, are not in the flesh but in the Spirit,

if in fact the Spirit of God dwells in you. Anyone who

does not have the Spirit of Christ does not belong to him.

But if Christ is in you, although the body is dead because

of sin, the Spirit is life because of righteousness. If the

Spirit of him who raised Jesus from the dead dwells in you,

he who raised Christ Jesus from the dead will also give life

to your mortal bodies through his Spirit who dwells in you.

ROMANS 8:9–11

CHAPTER 6

Spirit in Control: A Picture of Power

Every good thing God wants to shower on your life comes through the instrumentality of the Holy Spirit. Everything. The fruit of the Spirit, understanding of God's Word, love of worship, strength in a trial, grace to forgive, compassion for the lost, comfort in heartache, boldness in witnessing, power in ministry—all of this is yours when you live the Christian life in the Spirit's power. And conversely, none of it is yours when you attempt to live the Christian life any other way. Without the Holy Spirit, God has made no other provision for you to live the Christian life.

The Holy Spirit *is* the power. Galatians 2:20 says, **I have been crucified with Christ. It is no longer I who live, but Christ who lives in me.** There is no Christian life apart from Christ in you, and Christ is only in you by His Holy Spirit. Jesus told His disciples that if He went away, the Comforter would come. In John 14:16–17, Jesus says that the Holy Spirit would be in them forever. He will be in you. That's the promise of the Holy Spirit— not Jesus by your side talking to you, but His Holy Spirit *in* you, actually living out the Christian life through you.

Yes, with our will we can respond obediently to what we know pleases God—like worshipping, and walking with, and working for Christ, but even in the middle of that, the power to live the Christian life is **Christ in you, the hope of glory,** as Colossians 1:27 says. That's why Jesus said to the disciples in Acts 1:8, "Just get in a room and wait for the Holy Spirit to come. Do not pass Go, do not collect $200." The disciples probably wanted to get a plan together for building the church. *Can't we work on the brochures?* But Jesus told them to wait for the Holy Spirit. He knew they didn't have the capacity to do anything in their own power. **But you will receive power when the Holy Spirit has come upon you, and you will be my witnesses.** "When you have the Holy Spirit," He said, "you'll be able to do it all."

The Christian life is yieldedness to the Spirit of Christ living His life in you.

In this chapter, I want to remind you about what the Bible says about the Holy Spirit and how you can experience the ongoing, indwelling, overcoming presence of the Holy Spirit in your life today and what to do when you don't.

What We Know about the Holy Spirit

Last time I checked, it was truth that sets you free. So let's be reminded of some critical theology regarding the ministry of the Holy Spirit.

The Spirit Is God

Every bit as much as the Father and the Son, the Holy Spirit eternally exists as a distinct and separate person, yet one with the Trinity. Now, I don't understand the doctrine of the Trinity; all human illustrations fall short. I remember having the Trinity explained to me as water. It can be liquid, and it can be solid like ice, and it can be vapor. No, no, that's not really it. Well, it's like an egg, others explained. It's like the shell and the white and the yolk—no, no. It's a mystery. I think it's good to accept that there are mysteries in the Bible. We get too easily arrogant, overly clever, and man-centered when we think we've got the answer to mystery.

> *Without the Holy Spirit, God has made no other provision for you to live the Christian life.*

Deuteronomy 29:29 says, **The secret things belong to the LORD our God, but the things that are revealed belong to us.** God has not fully explained how the doctrine of the Trinity fits together (as if we could grasp it even then), but He has given us glimpses into this mystery throughout His Word.

Trinity means tri-unity. Three in one: Father, Son, and Holy Spirit. Deuteronomy 6:4 points us to the Father, **Hear, O Israel: The LORD our God, the LORD is one.** Affirming His place in the Trinity, Jesus said in John 10:30, **"I and the Father are one."** And then if you remember the baptism of Jesus in Luke 3:22, as Jesus came out of the water, the Spirit descended in the form of a dove, and a voice from heaven said, **"You are my beloved Son; with you I am well pleased,"** affirming all three persons of the Trinity. This was also done in Matthew 28:19, **"Go therefore and make disciples of all nations, baptizing them in the name of the Father and of the Son and of the Holy Spirit."**

You may ask, "James, why are you so insistent on this point that the Spirit is God?" Because Scripture is. Repeatedly, Scripture refers to different attributes of the Spirit as verifying His deity.

The Spirit Is Called by the Names of God

In 1 Corinthians 6:11, He is called **the Spirit of our God.** In Acts 16:7, He is called **the Spirit of Jesus.** In Romans 8:15, He is called **the Spirit of adoption,** which means He participates in applying salvation.

The Spirit Has the Attributes of God

Because we were created in the image of God, man mimics some of God's characteristics, but there are three character traits that *only* describe God. They are the three omni's: omniscient, omnipotent, omnipresent.

The Holy Spirit is omniscient. He knows everything. First Corinthians 2:11 says, **For who knows a person's thoughts except the spirit of that person, which is in him? So also no one comprehends the thoughts of God except the Spirit of God.**

Whatever you know about God was taught to you by the Spirit of God who is in you. We can't figure out anything about God on our own.

The Holy Spirit is also omnipresent. Psalm 139:7–8 says, **Where shall I go from your Spirit? Or where shall I flee from your presence? If I ascend to heaven, you are there! If I make my bed in Sheol, you are there!** Can you ever run away from God? If we could bring Jonah in to testify, he'd set us straight. You can't outrun God; He's everywhere.

The Holy Spirit is omnipotent. Job admits, **The Spirit of God has made me, and the breath of the Almighty gives me life** (Job 33:4). So the Spirit of God had a specific role in creation itself.

The Spirit Is Like . . .

When we encounter something beyond our ability to describe, we often try to compare it to something we know. As we study Scripture, we see God making Himself known in familiar pictures. For example, God says He's a mountain (Psalm 125:2), a king (Psalm 95:3), a shield (Psalm 18:2). All of these are pictures of the Father. Jesus made Himself known in pictures too. He said He's a vine (John 15:1), a door (John 10:9), the bread of life (John 6:48). And so it is true of the Holy Spirit. If we want to know what the Holy Spirit is like, here are five ways He makes Himself known to us.

A dove. Like we read above in Luke 3:22, Matthew 3:16 tells us, **And when Jesus was baptized, immediately he went up from the water, and behold, the heavens were opened to him, and he saw the Spirit of God descending like a dove and coming to rest on him.** This concept that the Spirit is like a dove appears in all four Gospels. So popular is this picture that the dove has become the universal symbol of the Holy Spirit. Leviticus 12:6 tells us the dove was one of the very few sacrifices acceptable to God in the Old Testament because of its purity.

Fire and wind. Acts 2:1–3 describes, **When the day of Pentecost arrived, they were all together in one place. And suddenly there came from heaven a sound like a mighty rushing wind, and it filled the entire house where they were sitting. And divided tongues as of fire appeared to them.** There's some debate about what exactly they saw, but the Holy Spirit is definitely described here as fire and wind.

This isn't the first time the Spirit is compared to fire. Isaiah 4:4 says that the Holy Spirit is **a spirit of burning.** Exodus 24:17 says,

The appearance of the glory of the LORD was like a devouring fire. John the Baptist promised that when Jesus came He would baptize with the Holy Spirit and fire (Luke 3:16). Again, the concept here is the Holy Spirit as a purifier.

I love this picture of the Holy Spirit as wind. We have a lot of wind in Chicago. The trees are blowing all the time. But here's the thing about wind—you never see it. You only see its effects. It's the same with the Spirit. We never see Him; we only see what He does. Jesus, talking to Nicodemus, said in John 3:8, **"The wind blows where it wishes, and you hear its sound, but you do not know where it comes from or where it goes. So it is with everyone who is born of the Spirit."** I've seen the Holy Spirit's effect in so many people, especially in our church. I've seen God changing them and challenging them, stretching them and growing them. I've never seen the Holy Spirit, but I've seen His powerful wind blowing through people's lives.

> *I've never seen the Holy Spirit, but I've seen His powerful wind blowing through people's lives.*

Oil. The pouring of oil is a picture of the Holy Spirit when anointing someone. Oil was used as a symbol of God's blessing and favor. When Aaron became a priest in Exodus 29:7, the people were instructed to take oil, pour it on his head, and anoint him. When Samuel chose first Saul and then David to be king, the first thing he did was to anoint them with oil (1 Samuel 9:16; 16:13). Acts 10:38 recalls how **God anointed Jesus of Nazareth with the Holy Spirit and with power.** It's a beautiful picture of the favor of God washing over someone. It is an extravagant blessing as the oil covers the head. It's a picture of the fullness of the Holy Spirit in our lives.

From the Lives of the First 120 Followers of Christ: A Picture of God's Power

Acts 2–4

If Christianity had been left up to the disciples, it would have dried up and died shortly after they watched Jesus ascend into the clouds. It would have lasted a couple of weeks at best, and then their lack of power would have ended in disillusionment. Spiritual fervor would have been a distant memory of "something special" but short-lived. "Why can't we make this work?" would haunt their thinking.

But history testifies that is *not* what happened. The eleven disciples, along with Jesus' earthly mother and brothers, formed the core of 120 people who could not and would not deny that something supernatural had occurred in the life, death, resurrection, and ascension of Jesus. Furthermore, something supernatural had occurred in *them* when they believed He was who He claimed to be—Messiah, Savior, Lord, *God!* Somehow they had a sense that they were living at the hinge point of history. But once Jesus had left the earth, they didn't know what to do other than what He had told them to do—wait.

A few days earlier Jesus' promise had sounded like a riddle, **"It is to your advantage that I go away, for if I do not go away, the Helper will not come to you. But if I go, I will send him to you. And when he comes, he will convict the world concerning sin and righteousness and judgment"** (John 16:7–8).

But with that promise came the secret to this new life. **"You will receive *power* when the Holy Spirit has come upon you, and you will be my witnesses"** (Acts 1:8, emphasis added). These 120 people had repented of their sin, confessed Him as their Lord and Savior, and now God gave them the supernatural thing that they needed to bear His name—He gave them power. They had new strength breathed into them. Individuals doing business with God were connected individually to the power of the universe.

Did anyone notice? These Spirit-filled people were the talk of the town! What happened to them? One day they are hiding and running and denying they even know Christ, and the next they are standing on the street corner shouting the good news. Where did this boldness, eloquence, and authority come from? Same source as it comes from today. Every day we're presented with a new opportunity for Him to fill us with His life so that we can experience God's power in a way we never could apart from Him.

What was the result? When these uneducated, unsophisticated, insecure followers of Jesus were filled with the power of God's Spirit, Acts 17:6 says that they **turned the world upside down.**

The world is still turning on the power of God at work in every Spirit-filled follower of Christ.

Water. And then, as we've been studying in this book, water is a picture of the Holy Spirit. This is a fantastic metaphor that Jesus Himself framed in John 7:37: **On the last day of the feast, the great day, Jesus stood up and cried out, "If anyone thirsts, let him come to me and drink. Whoever believes in me, as the Scripture has said, 'Out of his heart will flow rivers of living water.'" Now this he said about the Spirit, whom those who believed in him were to receive.**

To fully identify with this picture, you have to put yourself in the temple in Jesus' day at the time of that feast, which was the Jewish thanksgiving holiday named Sukkot (Festival of Tabernacles) that took place at the end of the dry season. As we learned in chapter 1, Israel had two seasons, wet and dry. If they didn't get rain in the spring and fall, they didn't eat the next year. So a big part of Sukkot was asking God for rain again next year. At the climax of this week of thanksgiving, the last day of the feast, the crowds thronged the temple in Jerusalem for the water ceremony where they would chant prayers for God to bring rain for the next year. Into this crowded scene walked Jesus.

This was the context for Jesus' bold invitation. Just imagine as the people cried for rain, Jesus shouted His offer,

Activities of the Holy Spirit

The Holy Spirit . . .
- is the source of all truth (1 John 5:6).
- is the author of Scripture (2 Peter 1:21).
- is the convicter of sin (John 16:8).
- is the provider of comfort (John 14:16).
- is the promoter of sanctification (1 Thessalonians 2:13).
- gives boldness to witness (Acts 4:31), grace to stand (Acts 9:31), courage to follow (Ephesians 3:16), hope to endure (Colossians 1:11).
- illumines God's Word (John 14:26).
- prays for God's people (Romans 8:26–27).
- advances God's agenda (John 16:13) in this world, in our country, in your church, your home, and in your life— that is the ministry of the Holy Spirit.

The Holy Spirit is doing a whole lot in this world!

"Are you thirsty? Come to Me!" We don't have to guess what His promise was about for "rivers of water to flow out of their hearts," since John 7:39 explains He was promising the Holy Spirit. It must have had a stunning impact! Jesus was promising life and revival to anyone who believed in Him.

The Spirit Is Active

You can be sure of this: the Holy Spirit isn't sitting around playing cards. He's active at this very moment. When we talk about all that the Lord is doing in our lives, in the church, and throughout the world, we're talking about the work of the Holy Spirit. We try not to overemphasize this person of the Trinity because Scripture tells us that the Holy Spirit's heart and mission is to make Jesus known (John 15:26). The Holy Spirit doesn't want to be in the spotlight. He wants the spotlight to be turned on the Son, Jesus Christ.

The Holy Spirit was active in the incarnation of Christ from the very beginning. When Mary was told by the angel that she was going to give birth to Jesus, Mary questioned, "How's this going to happen? How am I going to give birth to God's Son?" Luke 1:35 reports how the angel answered her: **"The Holy Spirit will come upon you, and the power of the Most High will overshadow you; therefore the child to be born will be called holy—the Son of God."** The mysterious, miraculous conception of the God-Man Jesus Christ was a ministry of the Holy Spirit.

The Spirit Is a Person

We must never accept the heresy that the Holy Spirit is just a force or an influence. The Arians taught in the early church that the Holy Spirit was the exerted energy of God, as in the result of God's work, but not a person. The Socians at the time of the Reformation taught the same thing. Later, theologians like Friedrich Schleier-macher, the Unitarians, and most neo-orthodox theologians deny the distinct personality and personhood of the Holy Spirit. In this century, the Mormons and the Jehovah's Witnesses do not believe that the Holy Spirit is God. They believe that He is the force of God or the influence of God, but they do not believe He is God.

So if somebody from one of these cults ends up on your front porch, can you prove the Spirit's personhood from Scripture? Let's think it through for a moment. If the Holy Spirit is really a person, He should have the attributes of personhood. As evidence of a soul, you need to have a mind, emotions, and a will. Does the Holy Spirit have these elements of personhood? Yes, He does.

First Corinthians 2:11 says that the Holy Spirit has *intellect*, the capacity to know. Ephesians 4:30 says that we can grieve the Holy Spirit, therefore, He has *emotions*. We can deeply sadden Him. First Corinthians 12:11 says that the Holy Spirit chooses which gift to give to believers, **as he *wills*** (emphasis added).

The Holy Spirit has a mind, emotions, and a will. The Holy Spirit is not just the *force* of God; He's not just *influenced* by God; He *is* God. The Holy Spirit is moving right now, using the Word of God to illuminate truth in our lives, convicting us of sin, calling us to righteousness, reminding us of the reality of judgment.

Every single thing we've talked about in relationship to the revival that God wants to bring to your life is coming through the Spirit of God. If you don't have the Holy Spirit's power, you'll never know a real, growing, genuine faith in God. At the end of the day, revival is more of the Holy Spirit actively working, stirring, and moving in you.

From Learning about
to Living in the Holy Spirit's Power

Ready to move now from doctrine to practice? We now have a foundation from which to build our relationship with God, the Spirit. In addition to knowing this truth, we need now to experience His personal ministry in our lives. I want so much for you to be transformed by His power. Without that, you will never realize the change you have been striving for.

> At the end of the day, revival is more of the Holy Spirit actively working, stirring, and moving in you.

One of the most important passages in all of Scripture regarding the Holy Spirit is Ephesians 5:18: **And do not get drunk with wine . . . but be filled with the Spirit.** This is the Christian life all in one message: "Be filled with the Spirit."

As a pastor, people ask me questions all the time about how to fix their lives. "I'm having a hard time loving my husband the way I should," someone says. "What should I do?" Answer: You need to be filled with the Spirit.

"I like my stuff more than I like my church," another declares. "Don't talk anymore about giving to God because I have no intention of giving up money that could buy me more stuff. What do I need?" Answer: You need to be filled with the Spirit.

"You talk all the time about the responsibilities and joys of serving Christ," someone tells me. "I know I should work in the church, but I really don't have the time. What do I need?" Answer: You need to be filled with the Spirit.

If you don't want what God wants for your life, you're not being filled by the Spirit. The Holy Spirit changes your priorities and your goals when He fills your life.

What Does It Mean to "Be Filled"?

Let's define what we mean by that Spirit filling. The Greek word is *pleroo*, which means to be "filled, controlled, intoxicated, thoroughly influenced." If you want to understand a word in Scripture, look at how it's used in other places in Scripture.

> As a child of God, you were given all of the Holy Spirit at conversion. The real issue is, Does the Holy Spirit have all of you?

In Luke 4:28, religious leaders listening to Jesus were "filled" with rage. In Acts 13:45, certain Jews were "filled" with jealousy at Paul and Barnabas' success. "Being filled" means to be overcome by a power greater than your own.

I know what it feels like to be filled with pain. The other day I was moving some things around in my closet in my bare feet. Somehow I caught my big toe on the end of a piece of furniture and it ripped the top half of my nail right off. In that agonizing moment I was no longer a person, or a pastor, or a husband, or a father—I was one, big, throbbing toe. I was "filled" with pain. When you're filled with something, that's all there is.

I know what it's like to be filled with joy. I remember our wedding day. Seeing Kathy coming down the aisle, I was "filled" with joy. There was nothing else—just that. I remember when each of our three children came into the world, and I held them for the first time. There was nothing but that joy. Being filled is being completely, totally, thoroughly captured.

That phrase in Ephesians 5:18, **be filled with the Spirit,** is packed with meaning.

1. Notice that "be filled" is a command. God doesn't ever say, "Why don't you give some thought to this." The good news is God

doesn't command things that aren't possible. God doesn't command you to do stuff and snicker to Himself, "It's never going to happen for her." That's not how He works. Every single person who has turned from his sin and embraced Christ by faith can be filled with the Spirit. Because God commands it, it is possible.

> *Sanctification is giving God total control of me, day after day being filled again.*

The work of God's Spirit is not limited to filling, but it is the only ministry of the Spirit in which we participate. Here's a fly-by of the Spirit's ministry to us at conversion: I looked to Jesus Christ by faith, the Spirit convicted me of sin, I turned from that sin, found the Lord at the cross, received Him for the forgiveness of sins, and the Spirit indwelt me. The Spirit then immersed me into the body of Christ (1 Corinthians 12:14). Then the Spirit sealed my place with God (Ephesians 1:13) so it can never be taken away. Nowhere in Scripture are you commanded to be indwelt by the Spirit or sealed by God's Spirit or baptized by God's Spirit. It happened by the Spirit's power. As a child of God, you were given all of the Holy Spirit at conversion. The real issue is, Does the Holy Spirit have all of you?

2. "Be filled" is also passive in the original language. If you remember your English grammar, passive tense refers to something that is acted upon. God is implied as the source of the filling, and we are the object acted upon. You can't fill yourself. Only God fills you with His Holy Spirit; what you can do is ask Him to do so.

3. "Be filled" in the original language is plural. Spirit-filling is not for the spiritually elite. It's not just for your pastor or your small group leader or anybody else you think has a direct connect with God. No, Spirit-filling is for all believers.

4. Finally, from Ephesians 5:18, "be filled" is repeated. The verb in the original tense is continuous action. Some translations write, "be *being* filled." Believers at Pentecost were filled once in Acts 2:4, and the same believers were filled again in Acts 4:8. Paul was filled with the Holy Spirit in Acts 9:17 and again in Acts 13:9. In contrast, we were baptized *once* into the body of Christ at conversion. That's when He comes to indwell us. One baptism, many fillings.

Now think about this. It's just a regular thing to be thirsty every day, isn't it? Drink a big glass of water, let a few hours go by, and you're thirsty again. That's the way it is with the Holy Spirit. You're filled with His power, you're living in a way that brings you and God great satisfaction and joy, but before long you're thirsty again—you need a refill of God's power from His indwelling Spirit every day. Sanctification is giving God total control of me, day after day being filled again.

I think we have all, at some time, taken a backward step in our spiritual lives. When we do, we forfeit the filling of the Holy Spirit. When I say or do something that deeply saddens the Holy Spirit, I forfeit His control. Because of this, I begin every day with a prayer, "Lord, fill me with Your Holy Spirit today." Sometimes throughout the day I've got to turn back to the Lord and say, "Forgive me for that thought. Forgive me for that word. Fill me again with your Holy Spirit. Control me now." To be really filled with the Holy Spirit, you have an almost tangible sense of the Holy Spirit controlling you.

Spirit-Filling Illustrated

It might surprise you, but the illustration the Holy Spirit gives us of His filling in Ephesians 5:18 is drunkenness. "Oh, that's crazy," you say. "We've got to come up with a different illustration." No, let's go with the one that God chose. Four separate times the Holy

Spirit inspired the writer of Scripture to use drunkenness as a picture of what it means to be filled with the Holy Spirit (Luke 1:15; Acts 2:4; Acts 2:13; Ephesians 5:18). These verses do not commend drunkenness, but they use it as a parallel.

If you've ever been drunk or observed someone under the influence of an inappropriate amount of alcohol, you know the first thing that happens to drunk people is that they lose control over their tongues. They say all kinds of outrageous things that bewilder and amuse people. Neither do they have control over their bodies. Policemen ask them to walk a line, but they can't do it because they don't have control over their bodies. They also have no control over their minds. Ask them a simple question and they stumble through an answer. People who are drunk have no control over their emotions. For no reason, they're fearful, angry, paranoid, and silly.

Want to be under the influence of something? Be controlled by the Spirit. God's Spirit wants to control your body, your emotions, and your mind. When you're controlled by the Spirit, He influences what you do and say. The Spirit of God can be an amazing guide, controlling what you think in your mind. If you're trapped in some negative pattern of thinking—anger, resentment, bitterness, frustration, impatience, fear, or worry—the Spirit of God can direct what your mind dwells upon. How desperately we need the Spirit of God to control our emotions. When the Spirit is in control, life is a whole lot better.

You'll Know You're Filled with the Holy Spirit When . . .

How do I know if the Holy Spirit is filling me now? That's a good question because you *can* know; it's not subjective. Paul gives

"Are You Filled with the Spirit?"— The Shantung Revival (1927)

As if political unrest and evacuation wasn't enough, missionaries in northern China had to face the probing questions that their fellow missionary, Marie Monsen, persistently asked them: "Have you been born again?" and "What evidence do you have of the new birth?"

As these relocated missionary teachers and doctors gathered for prayer and Bible study, God used these questions to prompt deep soul-searching. The humbled missionaries confessed and repented of sins and found reconciliation with God and one another. Some even realized they had never been saved, and they turned to Christ for the first time.

Missionary Charles Culpepper couldn't rest. He searched Scripture to understand what it means to be filled by the Holy Spirit. As he sincerely prayed to be filled, the Holy Spirit reminded him of past sins that had never been dealt with. He wrote letters asking for forgiveness. He sent stolen money back to his college alma mater and offered to return his diploma. But still he experienced no spiritual power in his work. He felt as if his heart was stone. "What is the matter, Lord?" he asked.

The Lord led him to Romans 2:17–25. God convicted him that he was a hypocrite and that the name of God was being blasphemed among the Chinese because of him. He awoke his wife, and they prayed all night. The next day, he confessed his pride to his fellow missionaries. He writes about what happened next:

> The Lord became more real to me than any human being had ever been. He took complete control of my soul—removing all hypocrisy, shame, and unrighteousness—and filled me with His divine love, purity, compassion, and power. During those moments, I realized my complete unworthiness and His totally sufficient mercy and grace . . . .
>
> The next day was Sunday, a new and wonderful day at our missionary church. I have never heard such praying or experienced such joyous fellowship as we had that day.

Students came back from the political displacement, only to be met by teachers who had been changed by God's Spirit. They began a series of meetings that prompted great conviction of sin in the students.

For ten days the services continued. By its end, more than fifteen hundred of the students had turned to or returned to God. God had brought a downpour of blessing, first through two penetrating questions for the missionaries, who in turn God used to impact a generation of students.*

*C. L. Culpepper, *Spiritual Awakening: The Shantung Revival* (self-published, 1982), 1–35.

us five confirmations of the filling ministry of the Holy Spirit in Romans 8:9–17. But let's get an overview first.

You, however, are not in the flesh but in the Spirit, if in fact the Spirit of God dwells in you. Anyone who does not have the Spirit of Christ does not belong to him. So conversely, anyone who *does* belong to Him *does* have the Spirit. If you're in Christ, you have the Spirit.

But if Christ is in you, although the body is dead because of sin, the Spirit is life because of righteousness. Even though you're physically going downhill,

> *The energy, the power, the strength, the comfort— all the things that you ask God for—are from the Spirit.*

spiritually you can be going up. **If the Spirit of him who raised Jesus from the dead dwells in you, he who raised Christ Jesus from the dead will also give life to your mortal bodies through his Spirit who dwells in you** (see also 2 Corinthians 4:16). The holiness that is happening in me is from the Spirit. The *life* of the Christian life is the Holy Spirit.

The energy, the power, the strength, the comfort—all the things that you ask God for—are from the Spirit. God does not dispense strength and encouragement like a druggist fills a prescription. When we ask for those things, God gives us His Spirit. The good things that happen in me are because of God's Spirit. My capacity to believe and to repent, the joy and peace that I receive—these are all ministries of the Holy Spirit.

Romans 8 continues, **So then, brothers, we are debtors, not to the flesh, to live according to the flesh. For if you live according to the flesh you will die** (vv. 12–13). Paul doesn't mean that we will just die physically because that wouldn't be much of a newsflash. Instead he's talking about dying spiritually. If you spend your lifetime feeding the flesh, then you don't really know the Lord and you'll die eternally.

But if by the Spirit you put to death the deeds of the body, you will live (v. 13). How do you put to death your sinful inclinations? How do you get over that private addiction? Answer: by the Spirit! How do you become a man of purity? How do you become a woman of righteousness? Answer: by the Spirit, you put to death the deeds of the body. The Spirit is the strength to do what is right.

Without the filling of the Holy Spirit, I'm like a piece of straw in one of those California firestorms. I've got no time left. *Well, I'm going to stand against that sin,* you may think. No, you had better run. You had better flee that temptation. Only the Spirit of God gives you the strength to do what's right.

"O.K., James," you say. "You've convinced me that I desperately need and want to be filled by the Holy Spirit. How do I know when I am?" Ask yourself the following five questions.

1. Is God Leading Me?

For all who are led by the Spirit of God are sons of God (Romans 8:14). So, are you one of God's children? If you are and you're filled with the Spirit, the Spirit of God is leading you. Everyone who is born of the Spirit is led by the Spirit. He directs you in what to say, what to do, and how to do it.

We had a phenomenal time with the pastors and ministry leaders who came again to our Straight Up ministry leadership conference this past year. At the end of the last service, this man approached me and said he had to tell me this story.

"We're from out of state and my wife really wanted to see Navy Pier while we were here. We skipped out of last night's session to go into downtown Chicago, but we got lost and couldn't find Navy

Pier. Finally, we went into a little coffee shop to order something and ask for directions.

"The waitress asked, 'What brings you to the area?' and I told her we were at a church conference up in the northwest suburbs.

"She asked, 'What church?' and I mentioned your name, James. And the woman burst out crying and ran away. She came back in a little while and I said, 'I'm sorry, I didn't mean to upset you.'

"'No, you didn't upset me at all. You see, I've just moved here, and I've been looking for a church. All I can tell you is that one day, one time on the radio, I heard this guy named MacDonald, and I've prayed for the last few days, "God, I have to know where this church is, and I have to know who this is."' She couldn't remember the radio station, or the program *Walk in the Word*, or anything."

So here's the point. This guy who skips out on the conference and gets lost is the answer to her prayer. You can't tell me that the Spirit of God did not lead them, even in their wrong turns and conference truancy. Isn't it good to know that even when I'm wandering, God is focused and leading the way?

By His Spirit, God sovereignly directs and works in our lives, leading us by His Spirit. This is the ongoing experience of the child of God. I don't have amazing things like that happen every day, but often every week I can point to a situation and say God led me in that. The Lord puts you in the right place at the right time to speak for Him. He leads you to a certain person. He puts the words in your mouth. This leading is evidence of being filled with the Holy Spirit. Is God leading you?

2. Is God Giving Me Confidence?

Romans 8:15 says, **For you did not receive the spirit** [attitude] **of slavery to fall back into fear.** Confidence is one of the overriding characteristics in the life of a person who is being filled with His Spirit.

Fear is what you had before Christ. If you talk to people who don't know the Lord, you see quickly that they're slaves to fear—fear of the future, fear of dying, fear of not having enough. People who don't know the Lord are filled with fear. But when the Spirit of God comes to live within you, He displaces that fear and fills that place with confidence instead.

We are blessed at our church to be firsthand witnesses to a family legacy. Our church staff is led by executive pastor, Joe Stowell IV. His dad, Joe Stowell III, former president of Moody Bible Institute, is our teaching pastor. And his grandfather, Joe Stowell II, age 94, lives nearby. I'll never forget when we broke ground on a new worship center, we asked Joe II to participate in the dedication service. He was quite frail as he walked out on the site. We put the microphone in his hand and asked him to dedicate the property in prayer. Talk about a transformation! As he began to pray his frail voice got so strong and confident and he "called down the thunder." He powerfully called upon God to bless this new ministry site. It was an awesome thing to observe.

How was he able to do this? It came from a lifetime of being filled with the Spirit. "We should trust the Lord. We don't know what's going to happen, but our confidence is in God." There is a growing confidence in the life of a person who is controlled or filled by God's Spirit. Are you experiencing that?

3. Am I Growing in Intimacy with God?

Romans 8:15 goes on, **But you have received the Spirit of adoption as sons, by whom we cry, "Abba! Father!"**

That's an amazing picture from the ancient world. If a man was not happy with his heirs, he could adopt a slave as a son and give him all the rights of sonship. What Romans 8:15 is saying is that as children of this world, redeemed by the precious blood of Jesus Christ, we have been adopted into God's family and we have been declared and treated as sons and daughters by Almighty God. The Spirit of God has been given to us by whom we cry out "Abba." That's a term of intimacy.

> To be filled with His Spirit is to desire and pursue a growing intimacy with God.

When the Spirit comes to live within us, He wants us to say, "Abba! Father!" Every culture has its own little phrase for this intimacy. Some kids say, "Daddy," others say, "Papa!" Whatever the lingo, it's tender. God's Spirit wants to bring you to that gentle place with the Lord.

When it comes to intimacy with God, women understand it big time and men are clueless. Men, we especially need to get to a place where we don't feel embarrassed in our private times with the Lord to call him, "Abba, Daddy! I need You! I love You, I'm hurting. I want You. I'm seeking You!" You might say, "I think I would feel a little weird calling out to God like that." All I'm saying is that the Spirit of God is trying to bring you to a place where you desire and pursue that kind of private intimacy with God.

What keeps us from doing that? Just pride. "I don't want to feel anything," we say. "I'll keep God at arm's length—this far and no further." There was a man standing beside me at a worship service this week who was stiff and stern the entire time. I'm telling you this was a fired-up worship service, and he stood there like a statue. I knew the Spirit of God wasn't controlling his heart because he was clearly not moving toward intimacy with God. The Spirit of God is trying to break down that pride in all of us. To be filled with His Spirit is to desire and pursue a growing intimacy with God.

4. Do I Feel Secure in Christ?

Romans 8:16 says, **The Spirit himself bears witness with our spirit that we are children of God.**

If there's one thing I hear from Christians over and over, it's doubts about their salvation. They begin to ask, "Am I really a Christian? Am I really saved?" Well, newsflash! It's a ministry of the Spirit of God to confirm to you the reality of your relationship in God's family. That's the ministry of God's Spirit to speak security in your heart.

> *He [God] wants to continuously fill you and satisfy you with Himself.*

Wouldn't you want your children to feel secure? How would Kathy and I feel if we came home and our three children were down in the basement whispering, "I'm not really sure if we're their children. Do we *really* belong to them?" We would grab them and hold them and tell them, "Of course you are ours." Parents would feel lousy if they heard that from their kids!

God feels the same way. He wants us to know that we are really His. One of the ministries of God's Spirit is to confirm to you the reality of your place in God's family, if in fact you are in God's family.

You may be asking, "Why don't I get all this?" You may be wondering why some of these ministries of the Holy Spirit are not a part of your spiritual experience. Here are a couple of biblical answers.

Sometimes we grieve the Spirit. Ephesians 4:30–31 says that we grieve the Spirit when we do what the Spirit doesn't want us to do.

Think about the sin in the mirror and that whole process we went through in chapter 3. Sin grieves the Spirit of God. We treat out-of-town guests better than we do the Holy Spirit of God who lives in us. The Spirit is sealed inside us, and when we choose sin it makes God's Spirit sad. If we go somewhere, He's going too. If we set our eyes upon sin, God's Spirit sees that too. We grieve the Spirit when we do things He doesn't want us to do.

Sometimes we quench the Spirit. We quench the Spirit when we don't do what the Spirit of God wants us to do. First Thessalonians 5:19 says, **Do not quench the Spirit.** It means don't extinguish the Holy Spirit's fire. I'm sad to say that I've seen this happen in my life. The Spirit directs me to do something and I say, "Nah." And each time He prompts me to respond and I refuse, His voice gets softer until I can't hear it anymore.

If you're not experiencing the confirming security of the Spirit of God in your life, if you've ever thought, *I don't even know if I am a child of God. These things aren't going on in my life,* then only repentance can restore the filling of the Holy Spirit in you.

5. Do I Draw My Identity from Christ?

Romans 8:17 says, **And if children, then heirs—heirs of God and fellow heirs with Christ.** Do you know how rich you are? An heir is someone who has the rights to everything that belongs to the father. Someday all that belongs to our heavenly Father will be ours. We live like paupers when we're children of the King because we're not experiencing the filling ministry of the Holy Spirit. To be filled with the Holy Spirit is to have a constant reminder in my life of the unsearchable riches of Christ and all that belongs to me as a blood-bought child of Almighty God. That's my identity as an heir and a joint-heir with Christ. You ask, "Why don't I feel more wealthy?" That reflects the lack of the Holy Spirit's filling of your life. "I think I've lost some of that," you say. Well, start again. You don't have to earn the Holy Spirit's filling; you just have to be willing and ask. God wants to fill you with His Spirit.

How to Be Filled with the Holy Spirit

Do you recognize your need as a follower of Jesus to be filled with the Holy Spirit? If your answer is yes, do the following three things and you most certainly will be.

1. Repent of All Known Sin

Do what we talked about in chapter 3 on a regular basis. Identify the sin in the mirror. If you discover anything that you're harboring, anything you're holding back, anything that's in the way— it's got to go. It grieves God's Spirit. Apply the exercises at the end of chapter 4 on repentance. Get beyond superficial confession and take the sin that grieves God's Spirit to a place of true repentance.

Some of you know the Lord, but you've been living a carnal Christian life for many years—not one day filled with the Spirit because of something you will not let go of or something that you won't do. You've got to be current with God's Spirit to be filled with God's Spirit. Keep in mind that you can't fool God. It's not a matter of rattling off a couple of token prayers. God knows your heart. Ask Him, **Search me, O God, and know my heart! Try me and know my thoughts! And see if there be any grievous way in me** (Psalm 139:23).

2. Ask God to Fill You

When you have dealt with all known sin through repentance, ask God to fill you with His Spirit. Open your hands and say,

"Come and fill me. Lord, I want to be controlled by You. I want to know Your fullness in my life to a greater degree than ever before by Your Holy Spirit. I see my need, so come and fill me now."

> *God has provided no other way for you to successfully live the Christian life apart from His Spirit filling you every moment of every day. The good news is: He promises unlimited refills.*

I love my children, and I love to give gifts to them. If we know how to give good gifts to people we love, how much more will God give the Holy Spirit to those who ask. Matthew 7:11 and Luke 11:13 reiterate this truth. If as earthly fathers we know how to give good gifts to our children, **how much more will your Father who is in heaven give good things to those who ask Him!**

3. Believe that He Has Filled You

John 14:13 affirms, **"Whatever you ask in my name, this I will do, that the Father may be glorified in the Son."** Matthew 9:29 promises, **"According to your faith be it done to you."** Refuse to doubt. Don't let your heart be filled with unbelief. Believe that God's Spirit has filled you. Express your faith to God. If you have dealt with all known sin as a follower of Jesus Christ and then prayed asking God's Spirit to fill you, He has done it!

Continuous Revival

The Holy Spirit wants to be continually filling you, empowering you with all the intensity and life and joy that is His to give. It's like putting your hand under a stream of water rushing out of a faucet. He wants to continuously fill you and satisfy you with Himself.

His Spirit is where the power comes from to live in a place of continuous revival with God. God has provided no other way for

you to successfully live the Christian life apart from His Spirit filling you every moment of every day. The good news is: He promises
unlimited refills.

Downpour

As I write this, it's beginning to rain outside. Isn't that cool?
Remember our downpour verse from Hosea 6:3: **Let us know; let
us press on to know the Lord; his going out is sure as the dawn;
he will come to us as the showers, as the spring rains that water
the earth.**

What started outside my window as a drizzle has now become
a downpour. The puddles on the roads are splashing up—it's an
out-of-control rain! That's the way God is to the person who comes
to Him for revival. He fills us, controls us, and empowers us. He is
the one who quenches our thirst. He is the one who fills up what's
missing. He is the one who satisfies our deepest longings. He is
the one who brings and sustains a continuous revival in our lives.
That's what the Holy Spirit is doing in the lives of those who follow the path of continuous revival that we have detailed in these
chapters. That's what He is doing in the lives of those of us who are
pressing on to know the Lord.

Come, come Lord Jesus; come to us like the rain.

ACTIVATE

For most of this chapter we've been learning that it's only
through the Holy Spirit's power that we will continue to experience
a downpour of spiritual blessing in our lives. The key is being filled
by the Holy Spirit on a daily—even moment-by-moment—basis.
Two things keep that from happening in your life: the first is grieving the Spirit—when you do things that sadden Him. The second

is quenching the Spirit—when you don't do what He's asked you to do.

1. *Grieving the Holy Spirit.* Since your salvation, the Holy Spirit is in you—once and for all. He goes where you go; He sees what you see. He hears what you say. So, be careful not to grieve God's Spirit (see Ephesians 4:30).

The word *grieve* literally means "to cause pain or sorrow." When we do things that are not pleasing to the Lord, it makes Him sad. Many things fall into this category, but Ephesians 4:29–30 targets one primary way we grieve the Holy Spirit. Read this passage in your own Bible.

- What is the common way that we often deeply sadden the Lord?
- How are you doing that right now?
- What should you do now that you see it?

2. *Quenching the Holy Spirit* (not doing the things He tells me to do). "Quench" means "to snuff out, douse, cool down, trim back." To quench God's Spirit is to extinguish His intended result. First Thessalonians 5:19 makes this direct command: **Do not quench the Spirit.** How do we put out His fire in our hearts? By ignoring and resisting His direction.

- What specific issue has the Spirit been talking to you about that you have ignored?
- What is He saying?
- Up until now, how have you resisted His Word?
- Deal with it right now before you quench His voice.

Deal with these two areas aggressively. Ignoring or resisting the Lord leads you back to that barren wasteland. By listening to God's Spirit and choosing not to grieve or quench, I allow that reviving work of the Lord to continue unhindered in me.

By confessing the inevitable moments when I foolishly grieve and quench God's Spirit as soon as they occur, I welcome the filling of the Holy Spirit and avoid another long journey into carnal living and the spiritual wasteland I have worked so hard to leave behind.

ELEVATE

Holy Spirit of God, thank You for filling my life with You. You are in control of all that I am—my thoughts, my actions, my words, and my feelings. Thank You, Spirit of God. I am now living under the downpour of Your power and strength and blessing, and I thank You for the riches of Your mercy. In the precious name of Jesus. Amen.

REPLICATE

Our key verse for this chapter has been Ephesians 5:18, **And do not get drunk with wine, for that is debauchery, but be filled with the Spirit.** Verse 19 is critical to keeping the downpour of revival flowing: **Addressing one another in psalms and hymns and spiritual songs.**

It's called *fellowship!* When we are filled with the Spirit, we talk about the things that fire up our faith. You can't keep quiet when you're learning about how great God is and what He's done in your life lately. The Holy Spirit loves it when we do this.

Need a conversation starter for your next time of friendly fellowship? Read Romans 8:9–17 again and review with a friend the five verifications that the Holy Spirit is filling you right now.

1. Lately God has really impressed upon me . . . . (v. 14).
2. God is giving me a new confidence so that . . . . (v. 15).
3. God has been drawing me closer to Himself in these areas . . . . (v. 15b).

4. You know, I used to struggle in my assurance of this _____ _____, but now He's given me real security in knowing this _____. (v. 16).

5. You'll never believe it, but I no longer get my sense of identity from . . . . (v. 17).

Pick one of these five evidences and share with someone today or tomorrow a time in your life when you clearly knew the Spirit was in control. The Holy Spirit will be listening in—and cheering you on!

Downpour

Here where self and sin and sadness have displaced
    the oil of gladness,
Here in barren, desert madness, weary and dry,
Cannot run or walk, I'm crawling but through shame
    I hear You calling,
Clouds of mercy, raindrops falling.

Downpour. I need a downpour.
Come, come like the rain; wash every stain;
    fall upon me, Jesus,
River of God, flooding with joy, well up in me, Jesus.

Into my heart's desolation flows the water of salvation;
Fill this lowly wasteland with the shower from above.
Only You can quench my thirsting;
    fill until my heart is bursting.
Jesus, ever be the first thing.

Downpour. I need a downpour.
Come, come like the rain; wash every stain;
    fall upon me, Jesus,
River of God, flooding with joy, well up in me, Jesus.*

*Words by James MacDonald; Music by Andi Rozier, © HARVESTsongs 2005.

Epilogue

Everything that has happened in your heart as you have read this book and activated its truth in your heart through the application exercises has been about crisis. From the beginning I told you that downpours begin with a crisis. A crisis of returning to God. But what do we do when the crisis is over?

You may be saying, "James, I've dealt with my sin in view of God's holiness, I've repented and made restitution and reveled in the grace of the cross. I'm at a better place with God than I have been for a long time, but how do I keep it going? How do I keep the river flowing? How do I keep the downpour falling, and how do I keep flourishing in my relationship with Christ? And what if I struggle or stumble or fall?"

Those are the right questions to be asking now. Let me give you a simple answer: *When you* falter *in the process of continuous revival, you must return to the crisis.* Live every moment of every day in continuous revival through the filling ministry of the Holy Spirit. Inevitably you will stumble. When you do, go back through the chapters and review these five pictures:

1. God on the Throne: A Picture of Holiness
2. Sin in the Mirror: A Picture of Brokenness
3. Self in the Dirt: A Picture of Repentance
4. Christ on the Cross: A Picture of Grace
5. Spirit in Control: A Picture of Power

They are a proven road to revival. If you lose your way, retrace your steps. I cannot overemphasize this point: When you fail in the process, return to the crisis. Personal revival is always available for every follower of Jesus Christ. When you realize you've drifted away from a passionate pursuit of Christ, turn around, repent of the sin God shows you in the mirror, and take hold of the grace freely bestowed on all who believe.

When you falter in the process of continuous revival, you must return to the crisis.

This week, I read the testimonies of twenty well-known Christian leaders in the book *They Found the Secret*. Though they led very different lives and had very diverse personalities, the spiritual lives of Hudson Taylor, Amy Carmichael, Oswald Chambers, Charles Finney, and the other men and women whom God greatly used, all expressed a common pattern. One witness after the next testified to the crisis of the Christian life leading them to experience the reality of the joy and power of the Spirit-filled life. In their lives and in yours and mine, the path that leads from the barren, dry wasteland of a spiritual life to the abundant, overflowing, life Jesus promised is *the filling of the Holy Spirit.*

As you know, revival doesn't come from trying harder or wanting it more. If it did, the church would be ablaze with fervent, obedient, fired-up worshippers. No, only one thing keeps the portals of heaven open, and it's not anything that we can pump up in our flesh. Downpours come when you are standing under the supernatural flow and power of God's Spirit. It's Christ in you who is your hope of glory; it's Christ in you who satisfies and refreshes. Being fully and gloriously controlled by His Spirit is the secret of lasting, transforming joy that produces a deeply satisfying downpour.

I praise God for the work He has done in your heart in accordance with the effort you have expended in personally applying the truths of these pages. More important than the truth in this book is what flows from the truth of God's eternal Word.

Throw away your umbrella and enjoy the rain!

Live every moment of every day in continuous revival through the filling ministry of the Holy Spirit.

At the beginning of our study, we agreed on five promises. Read the following and adapt or confirm in prayer that these promises continue to be your desire as you seek a lifetime of continuous revival.

From this date forward _____, I promise:

- that I will be dissatisfied with anything less than a genuine personal experience with God.
- that I will set God's Word high above human teaching and will handle it with the respect it deserves.
- that God will have access to every area of my life.
- that the principles I've learned in this book about "Sin in the Mirror" and "Self in the Dirt" are about me and God alone.
- that this truth about God's holiness, my sinfulness, the need for repentance, God's grace, and the filling of the Holy Spirit will always be a part of my spiritual life.

I promise!

Acknowledgments

I've always said that the Christian life is not a solo sport, and I am more convinced of this than ever. Writing a book drives that lesson home very persuasively. I'm never sure if people take time to read these statements of gratitude; I only know I must take time to express them. I am thankful certainly for what the following people have done, but even more so for what they are to my life and ministry.

- Thanks to our ministry partners at LifeWay and Broadman & Holman—John Kramp, Bill Craig, Mark Marshall, Jeff Good, Leonard Goss, Claude King. More than effective publishers, you are partners in the passionate pursuit of God.

- Thanks to Robert and Bobbie Wolgemuth. More than representation with integrity, you love Christ so obviously and contagiously.

- Thanks to Kathy Elliott, my assistant for eighteen years. But more than that, you are my friend and a faithful, fruitful follower of Jesus Christ.

- Thanks to Barb Peil, my tireless writing partner. More than hard work and long hours, you have joyfully listened and studied until our individual voices are indiscernible and together more powerful.

- Thanks to David Jones, my partner in research and biblical reflection. More than accurate interpretation, you put your whole humble heart into your work, which supports my work. We are the sum for God that is greater than the parts.

- Thanks to Trei Tatum and Lynda Nickels. More than Downpour staff members, you work so tirelessly in our church to carry the waters of God's blessing to other dry places, coming soon to cities across North America.

- Thanks to the elders at Harvest Bible Chapel. More than just my authority and accountability, you are my dearest friends and supportive co-laborers. You help me keep first things first and ensure that my heart is gladly tethered to one place and one people as my highest calling.

- Thanks to Mart and Rick DeHaan and Janine Nelson of RBC Ministries who undergird and greatly extend the mission of Walk in the Word. More than expanding my vision for multiple messengers with one message, you have modeled and given to me a greater joy in serving Christ.

- Special thanks to Kathy, my loyal wife and closest confidant, and to my three kids, Luke, Landon, and Abby—so close now to lives on your own—for enduring a Christmas season with deadlines looming large. You are more than just a pastor's family. Christ in and through each of you is the cloud of mercy that rains continuous joy and laughter upon our home.

HE WILL COME TO US LIKE THE RAIN
downpour
A watershed event for Christians
Minneapolis, Minnesota
November 3-4
Coral Gables, Florida
November 17-18
JAMES MACDONALD
JOE STOWELL
CRAWFORD LORITTS JR.
for more information
call 1.800.254.2022
or visit www.lifeway.com/jamesmacdonald
LifeWay
Biblical Solutions for Life
ADULT
HE WILL COME TO US LIKE THE RAIN

The landscape of our lives has become dry and scorched.

But heaven is bursting with the blessings God wants to rain

down upon us. Not a drizzle, but a deluge. With its powerful

call to revival, **James MacDonald's** new study leads believers

to lift up their eyes and return to the Lord. Because when we

do, He will heal us … revive us … and restore us. So if your

church is thirsty for spiritual renewal, get ready to …

Soak it in.